# 25 Walks in New Jersey

# 25 Walks in

by Kevin T. Dann

Photographs by the author

# New Jersey

Rutgers University Press

New Brunswick, New Jersey

Library of Congress Cataloging in Publication Data

Dann, Kevin T., 1956–
    25 walks in New Jersey.

    Includes index.
    1. Hiking—New Jersey—Guide-books.   2. Parks—
New Jersey.   3. Forest reserves—New Jersey.
4. New Jersey—Description and travel—1951—
Guide-books.  I. Title.
GV199.42.N5D36        917.49        81–5841
ISBN 0–8135–0935–1 (pbk.)        AACR2

Copyright © 1982 by Rutgers,
The State University of New Jersey

Manufactured in the United States of America

*To Catherine Dann*

# Contents

# Introduction

# Introduction

Twenty-five walks in *New Jersey*? I imagine this cry of
disbelief being issued by many people, walkers and non-
walkers alike—and perhaps for this very reason a book
such as this serves a purpose. For many people, especially
travelers who see the state from the New Jersey Turnpike,
New Jersey is the epitome of an industrial metropolis.
Many who live (or have lived) in New Jersey, however,
have an altogether different image: windswept beaches,
rolling hill country, steep talus slopes, broad green river
valleys, beaver ponds, and dense cedar swamps—these
are all part of New Jersey's landscape. There is no better
way to appreciate and understand this landscape fully
than to walk through it, and these walks are presented in
that spirit of coming to know, and hence more deeply
appreciate, the land.

The walks are arranged in sections according to different natural areas or regions. These regions are actually
subdivisions of larger areas known as physiographic provinces—areas having similar rock types, geologic structures, and geologic histories. The physiographic provinces
and the associated natural regions in New Jersey are as
follows.

### The Ridge and Valley Physiographic Province

The Ridge and Valley Physiographic Province extends
from the lowland of the Saint Lawrence River south some
1,200 miles to northern Alabama. Sometimes called the
Folded Appalachians, this province is composed mainly of
folded and faulted sedimentary rocks of early Paleozoic
age. Differential erosion of resistant sandstone, quartzite,
and conglomerate and the less-resistant shale and lime-

2

stone has resulted in a series of nearly parallel valleys and ridges. In New Jersey, the Ridge and Valley Province consists of the Kittatinny Valley, Kittatinny Mountain, and the Minisink (or Delaware) Valley. The three walks in this province are on the *Kittatinny Ridge*, the Endless Mountain of the Lenni Lenape Indians.

## New England Upland Physiographic Province

The New England Upland is the remnant of what was once a dramatic mountain system. Today, after millions of years of erosion, the roots of this mountain system survive as a series of broad ridges and narrow valleys beginning in northern New England and continuing south to Reading, Pennsylvania on the west and Manhattan Island on the east. The massive ridges of the New England Upland are composed of resistant metamorphic rocks such as gneiss and granite while the valleys are underlain by softer shale and limestone. The Reading Prong of the New England Upland extends into New Jersey as the *Highlands*, which contains the oldest rocks found in the state.

## The Piedmont Physiographic Province

The Piedmont Physiographic Province stretches southwest from the Palisades along the Hudson River 1,000 miles to central Alabama. The Piedmont (literally "foot of the mountain") is gentle hill country: the farms of Bucks County, Pennsylvania, central Virginia, and a century ago, northeastern New Jersey, are all located on the Piedmont's loamy soils. In New Jersey the *Piedmont* consists of the Newark basin and its associated traprock ridges, the Palisades and the Watchung Mountains. The two walks under the *Delaware River Valley* are also located in the Piedmont.

*The Atlantic Coastal Plain Physiographic Province*

The Atlantic Coastal Plain Physiographic Province, which contains about 60 percent of New Jersey's total land area, stretches from Cape Cod to Mexico. It is characterized by its level relief and its unconsolidated layers of gravel, sand, and clay. In New Jersey, the province is usually defined as having two subdivisions: the Inner and Outer Coastal Plains. Although both regions appear similar, the sediments of the Inner Coastal Plain were largely deposited during the Cretaceous period and are higher in clay content than the sandier Tertiary deposits of the Outer Coastal Plain. The walks under the *Pine Barrens*, the *Atlantic Coast* (except Gateway National Recreation Area, which is at the edge of the *Inner Coastal Plain*), and *Cape May* are located on the Outer Coastal Plain.

Because the underlying geology influences topography, soil types, and even climate, it also has a direct influence on plant communities. These plant communities in turn order and define the visible landscape—be it a rocky ridge top, a barrier beach, or a salt marsh. Since these plant communities are largely defined by their most prominent components—trees—much of the description contained in each walk is devoted to characterizing and identifying the forest trees present. Each tree is identified only once, though it may occur along a dozen or more of the trails described in this book. If, while reading, you encounter a tree or shrub that is not identified, refer to the Identification Index at the back of the book; this will give you the walk in which a complete description appears. Since one picture is worth a thousand words, however, it is helpful to have a pictorial guide in learning to recognize the native trees and shrubs of the state. Standard references are *A Field Guide to Trees and Shrubs* by George A. Petrides (Houghton Mifflin Co., 1972) or the *Master Tree Finder* by May Watts (Nature Study Guild, 1963). Once one learns to recognize the various trees and shrubs, one can begin to infer things about the entire community of which they are a part—which wildflowers are likely to be present, which birds might breed there, the kinds of mammals that might be found, and so on.

New Jersey's plant, animal, and mineral resources have not gone untouched, but have been exploited by man for nearly three centuries. Since a key to understanding the present landscape is to know what the past human impacts have been, many of the walks—Great Falls, Wharton State Forest, Waterloo Village, and others—illustrate the theme of resource use. In some ways, it is the underlying theme of much of the state's history, and at times it is a dismal one. It is to be hoped that these walks can help us to learn more careful stewardship of our resources by allowing us to reflect upon our past use (and misuse) of them.

*Taking Care of the Land*

Hiking trails (and books that describe them), by promoting the areas they traverse, sometimes run the risk of simultaneously destroying them. It is imperative that these areas be protected and preserved. Each area has its own rules and regulations; please observe these rules, as they are meant for your safety and protection as well as that of the area itself. Where there are no posted regulations, please follow these courtesies:

Don't disturb plants or animals.
Don't smoke while hiking.
Leave the trail as if nothing had been there;
    carry out all litter.

*Using the Book*

All of the walks in this book require less than a day to complete, and many take less than half the day. The walking times indicated at the beginning of each walk are of course approximate and do not include time for lunch and rest stops. The walks are graded according to their level of difficulty (easy, moderate, difficult). The maps for each walk are schematic and often do not include auxiliary trails or certain landscape features. If you wish to obtain more detailed maps, stop at the area's visitor's center (whether an area has such a center is noted at the beginning of the walk). Topographic maps may be helpful for some of the longer walks; these are available from the following addresses (write for a state index):

Distribution Section, U.S. Geological Survey
1200 South Eads Street
Arlington, Virginia 22202

or

Bureau of Geology and Topography
Department of Environmental Protection
P.O. Box 1390
Trenton, New Jersey 08625.

If, as you walk the trails, you find the descriptions are no longer accurate, please let the author know so that future editions can be corrected. Write him in care of the publisher.

# The Kittatinny Ridge

Looking south along the Delaware River from Mount Tammany (Arrow Island in foreground), Delaware Water Gap

# 1. High Point State Park

*Monument Trail*
Distance: 3½ miles (Moderate)
Walking time: 2 hours
Directions: Take NJ 23 north to High Point State Park
entrance. Turn right onto Kuser Rd., pass tollbooth, and
follow signs to High Point Monument. Park in lot near the
monument. A parking fee is charged from Memorial Day
to Labor Day.

In the extreme northwestern corner of New Jersey, along
the crest of the Kittatinny Mountains, lies the state's high-
est elevation: High Point. Atop the 1,803-foot summit is
High Point Monument, a 220-foot-tall monolith built of
New Hampshire granite and locally obtained quartzite.
This walk begins at this outstanding landmark, runs along
a 1,700-foot-high ridge, and then leads around an extensive cedar swamp.

During the summer you may climb to the top of the
monument for a spectacular view; however, the view
from the base of the monument is almost as impressive.
To the west lies the Minisink Valley and the Delaware
River, with the ridges of the Pocono Mountains towering
in the distance. Looking to the northeast one sees the
Catskill Mountains, while to the southeast lies the valley
of the Wallkill River. Southwest along the Kittatinny Ridge
several points may be seen: the Delaware Water Gap lying
forty miles away, Culver's Gap and Sunrise Mountain in
the middle distance, and in the foreground, Lake Marcia
and High Point Lodge. The lodge was formerly Col. An-
thony Kuser's residence; it was Colonel Kuser who gave
the land to the state in 1923.

Before you get on the trail, take one look to the north;
on this walk you will be following the ridge that lies di-

rectly in front of you, then descending to a valley that holds Cedar Swamp. The swamp appears as an island of conifers within the extensive deciduous woodland to the north.

As you descend the steps from the monument platform, the blue-blazed Monument Trail lies to your left. When you have located the trail, follow it north (turn right).

The exposed rock along the trail is Shawangunk conglomerate, which originated over 400 million years ago as fine sediments laid down in an ancient sea. The white quartz pebbles imbedded in the light-colored conglomerate rock were deposited by streams that drained into this sea. The level layers of sediments were lithified (became rock) and then folded, faulted, and finally uplifted millions of years later. The erosion-resistant conglomerate has been left as a ridge because the less-resistant sedimentary rocks adjacent to it have been worn away.

During the latest epoch of geological history, the Pleistocene, the ridge was stripped of its overlying soil by the glacial ice sheet which once covered much of northern New Jersey. This part of the ridge is still slowly regaining its soil mantle, and a few minutes spent exploring the bare rock along the trail will show how this soil-building process works.

The first plants to colonize the bare rock are crustose lichens; these appear as dark stains on the surface of the light-colored conglomerate. Lichens are actually a combination of a fungus, which provides anchorage, and an algae, which contains chlorophyll and can manufacture food for itself and its partner. This unique combination allows lichens to live in extremely harsh places such as this exposed rock. You may notice other lichens as you explore, some that are leaflike in shape and others that are branched like miniature trees. All of these lichens play an important soil-building role here on this bare rock, as they catch soil particles blown by the wind. When the lichens die, they add more material to the thin soil, allowing new plants to move onto the rock.

The next plants to arrive are the mosses, which find root in crevices in the rock where small amounts of soil have accumulated. These begin to make enough of a substrate that seeds from larger plants can take root. One of the first to do so is hairgrass, the sparse-looking grass seen scattered about the rock. Other grasses and a few species of fern join the hairgrass; most distinctive is the common polypody or rock polypody fern which spills out in evergreen mats over the rough rock. Rock polypody is readily identified by the way the leaflets are broadly attached to the main stem, and by the conspicuous round fruit dots on the underside of the leaflets.

Shrubs seen on the rock outcrops—blueberry, huckleberry, and sheep laurel in particular—eventually move in and shade out the smaller plants, creating more soil, and making way for the final stage of succession. To see this stage, continue along the trail and keep your eyes to the left. The forest here is composed of two trees that can survive the rigorous environment of this ridge top: scrub oak and pitch pine. The strong winds and icy winter conditions reduce the scrub oak to a thicket-forming shrub, and prune the windward side of the pitch pines so that they appear to be leaning uphill. The conditions for growth are so severe that seventy-year-old pitch pines may be only fifteen or twenty feet tall.

Located along this beginning section of trail are two small northern trees: striped maple and American mountain ash. The mountain ash is easily recognized from August to March by its clusters of small red fruits, and at other times of the year by its compound leaves with eleven to seventeen long, toothed leaflets. These fruits often remain on the tree all winter and are a favorite food at that time of the year for the strikingly colored evening grosbeak. Here at High Point the mountain ash is at the southern limit of its range.

The striped maple, another northern species, is a slender tree with green bark marked by vertical white stripes. Its three-lobed leaves are green on both sides, though slightly paler beneath. If you look closely at both the striped maple and the mountain ash, you'll see that deer have been browsing on their twigs. Further north, the fondness of the deer's cousin the moose for striped maple has given the plant the alternative name of moosewood.

Lake Marcia and High Point Monument, High Point State Park

The trail passes through the parking lot and enters the woods at the rear of the lot. The woods are predominantly chestnut oak, with some red and black oaks, and occasional hickories. Though less severe than the bare rock passed earlier, this and much of the rest of the Kittatinny Ridge are dry and windswept, conditions that the chestnut oak seems better adapted to than most other trees. Under the stunted chestnut oak canopy grows an understory of sassafras, black birch, and American chestnut sprouts, and below these is a shrub layer of huckleberry, blueberry, black chokeberry, sweet fern, and maple-leaf viburnum. Occasional white birch trees grow up between the jumbled rocks on the slope to the left.

As the trail leads north, the ridge narrows to a knife-edge, allowing vistas to the east one minute, to the west the next. The trail continues ¼ mile and then begins to descend from the ridge. Another ¼ mile further it reaches a gravel road; turn left here. Tall hemlocks tower over a wall of rhododendron which flanks the road. At one point, there is a break in this wall, and a low-lying ridge can be seen to the right. This ridge is underlain by red sandstone of the High Falls formation (a formation is a mappable rock unit and is usually named for some distinctive location where it is found). Like the Shawangunk conglomerate, the High Falls sandstone has resisted millions of years of erosion and today makes up much of the Kittatinny Ridge.

Soon the road comes to a fork (there is a bench on the left here); bear right. Almost immediately after you turn you will see the cedars viewed earlier from the monument. These are Atlantic white cedars, a tree commonly found along the edges of rivers and ponds in southern New Jersey, but confined to poorly drained swamps and bogs here in North Jersey. This slender conical tree has olive green foliage with tiny scalelike needles. The spherical cones are also tiny—about ¼ to ½ inch long. The gray, fibrous bark of the Atlantic white cedar is distinctive; it seems to twist its way up the trunk.

This cedar swamp had its origins during the close of the Ice Age, when glacial drift (rock material transported by the ice sheet) blocked a stream flowing between the two ridges and subsequently formed a pond that had no outlet. Slowly, over the last 12,000 years or more, this pond became a bog as it filled in with vegetation that formed a floating mat on top of the water. As more vegetation grew on top of the mat, plants on the underside died and fell to the bottom of the pond. Because of poor aeration, there was little decomposition of these plant remains, and layer upon layer of these remains—called peat—accumulated. With little plant matter decaying, the nutrients remained locked up in plant tissue rather than being recycled for other plants to use.

The lack of oxygen combined with the slow decay process creates an extremely acidic environment for plant growth, one that few plants can tolerate. Though the bog has matured to become a swamp with predominantly woody plants, some of the smaller plants that once covered the bog in its earlier stages are still visible. Sphagnum moss, its spongy leaves holding great amounts of water, forms hummocks throughout the swamp. On top of these sphagnum hummocks grow a number of curious insectivorous plants which can be seen along the road here. These plants obtain important nutrients they are unable to obtain from the sterile soil in which they grow—nitrogen, phosphorus, potassium, and others—from insects. The most conspicuous of these is the pitcher plant; it is identified by its tall, red-veined, purplish, tubular leaves which grow in a rosette from the base of the plant. These leaves become filled with water, making them traps for unwary insects. The inside of the leaf is very smooth, providing no foothold for the victims, and at the top of the leaf are downward-pointing hairs which help to move the insect down into the pool of water, but prevent it from moving up out of the trap. Once an insect drowns at the bottom of the pitcher, the plant secrets enzymes which digest it.

Another insect-eating plant seen here is the round-leaved sundew, although it is often overlooked because of its small size; the entire plant is only about two inches wide. Like those of the pitcher plant, its leaves have evolved to capture insects; however, the sundew's mechanism is a sticky secretion on the leaf hairs. After an insect becomes stuck, the leaf slowly folds over and digests it. It is often possible to see sundew leaves with the indigestible outer parts of the insects still adhering to them.

Just before the road swings left, look carefully to the right; the scrawny-looking evergreen tree leaning over the road is a black spruce. In northern New England and Canada, black spruce often forms dense stands in bogs, but here at the southern tip of its range it occurs as scattered individuals growing between the hemlocks and cedars. Some scientists believe that this and other isolated stands of black spruce are relics left from a time when the local climate was colder.

Bear left and follow along the edge of the swamp; the rhododendron and hemlock on the left contrast with the chestnut oak and low-bush blueberry on the right. The road passes a large upthrust conglomerate boulder on the right; a closer look at this boulder will reveal that the conglomerate is underlain by black shale or slate. The sediments that make up this slate were deposited during the late Ordovician period, about 450 million years ago.

The trail comes to another fork; bear left here to continue along the edge of the swamp. The rhododendron is joined by mountain laurel and swamp azalea, which combine to create a lovely floral display in June. Behind these shrubs grow cedars and occasional black spruce, while to the right grow bracken fern, scrub oak, and sheep laurel under a canopy of white and chestnut oaks. Scattered pitch pines grow on the low ridge beyond the oaks.

This corner of the swamp is more open than the area traversed so far: there are fewer trees, and the great banks of rhododendron seen earlier are absent. The trail swings left aroung the end of the swamp and then climbs a knoll that gives a nice view of the swamp when the leaves are not fully out. After passing one last area of dense cedars and hemlock, the trail emerges at a paved road; follow this road ¼ mile, past the picnic area, and then turn left and follow the road to the monument in order to return to your car.

# 2. Stokes State Forest

*Tillman Ravine*
Distance: 1½ miles (Easy)
Walking time: 45 minutes
Directions: Take Interstate 80 to Sparta exit. Go north on NJ 15 to US 206. Go north on US 206, 7 miles to sign for Boy Scouts camp and Stokes State Forest. Turn left and go 4½ miles to parking area (on left).

A visit to Tillman Ravine is like a return to some primeval forest: 100-foot hemlocks tower overhead as you walk along a pristine brook broken here and there by waterfalls and swirling pools. The hemlock boughs scatter the sunlight into hundreds of thin rays which dimly illuminate the forest floor. There is silence, with the only exception the sound of the rushing water of Tillman Brook.

Begin your walk at the parking lot, taking the trail to the left of the trail-map sign. This trail immediately enters a stand of red and white pine, planted in 1932 by the Civilian Conservation Corps. As you walk through the pines, see if you notice a change in temperature. When you do, look up: you've left the pines behind and entered a hemlock forest. The dense foliage of the hemlock allows little sunlight to enter, and combined with the moisture from the nearby brook, it creates an area of cooler air. Such an area is known as a microclimate, a small area with a climate distinctly different from that of its surroundings. Further north, where hemlocks are more common, this cool, moist microclimate is more readily found, but here in New Jersey, hemlocks must find deeply cut, often north-facing, ravines in which to grow.

As you walk along Tillman Brook, you may be impressed by the sheer size of the trees: some hemlocks here have been measured to be almost 4 feet in diameter, and 112 feet in height. Most of these larger trees are well over 100 years old, and some are as old as 160 years. How have these trees survived the cutting and burning that have affected most of New Jersey's landscape?

Hemlocks have traditionally been protected from the ax because the steep ravines in which they are found have been unfriendly territory for most woodsmen. But more than their location has kept these big hemlocks standing: their wood is of poor quality, and the rock-hard knots can chip the finest steel ax blade. Even today, the principal use for hemlocks is as wood pulp. It's fortunate that such a lovely tree has so little commercial value.

The other trees that you may see scattered through the hemlock forest are also more typical of cooler climes: yellow birch and American beech especially. If you look carefully for seedlings, however, you'll notice that young hemlocks are the most numerous. This is because once hemlock has become established, it tends to become the dominant tree unless disturbed. Such a forest is known as a climax forest, because it will continue to reproduce itself naturally. The tall mature hemlocks cast the deep shade that is preferred by their seedlings, but that is unfavorable to most others. In addition, the fallen hemlock needles tend to make the soil more acid, a condition that is also preferred by the young hemlocks.

After you cross the first wooden footbridge over Tillman Brook, look downstream to a maze of exposed hemlock roots. This tree was blown over during a storm in 1964. Hemlocks are often toppled by wind because their roots are shallow and cannot support the weight of such large trees in a high wind. A few yards further to your right, there is an abrupt outcrop of rock that appears to be made up of horizontal bands. These bands are actually layers of sand and mud which were deposited some 400 million years ago when this area was a broad river delta only slightly above sea level. About 250 million years ago, after these sediments had been lithified to become sandstone, they were contorted when much of New Jersey experienced a period of mountain building. Occasionally, the mountain-building forces were so great that rocks at the surface were fractured. This outcrop is a good example.

A short distance further, the brook is flanked by rhododendron. The moist air and acid soil make this a suitable spot for this more southern plant. Acid-loving herbaceous plants accompany the hemlock and rhododendron here: trailing arbutus, partridgeberry, Canada mayflower, and pink lady's slippers are most common.

The dampness of the ravine is evident along here in the lush growth of moss on the soil, rocks, and fallen logs. Even the usually silver gray trunks of the beech trees have a green hue from the moss. The high humidity is especially beneficial to one group of animals in Tillman Ravine: salamanders. These small animals are often overlooked because they spend much of their time beneath rocks and fallen logs. With some careful looking, the following species may be seen in this area: the slimy salamander, red-spotted newt, red-backed salamander, northern two-lined salamander, dusky salamander, and northern red salamander.

Continue along the ravine trail to where the brook runs through a break in a sandstone outcrop. Here the rock has again been folded to the point of fracturing, and one can

Rhododendron and ferns, Tillman Ravine

see that the brook has followed the path of least resistance along this break in the rock. The stream shoots along and over the Lower Falls. Just below the falls is the Teacup, an area in the sandstone that has been scoured out by the rocks and sand carried by the brook. Such circular, smooth-sided excavations in rock are called potholes. In times when the water is low, some of the rocks that helped to form the pothole can be seen lying at the bottom.

Actually, a whole series of potholes can be seen here. Just above the Teacup is a ledge where a pothole is beginning to develop. This small pothole will gradually be enlarged by Tillman Brook. Below the Teacup is a pothole that was breached when the front of it eroded away. This former pothole appears as a semicircle.

Continue along the trail as it follows the stream down through the hemlocks. Although the ravine is a place of great quiet, you'll hear certain distinctive sounds coming from the treetops. Chickadees and nuthatches, both of which feed on the seeds of the hemlock, are usually heard as they forage about. You may hear a peculiar sound which is not as familiar: a loud chattering "chir-r-r-r, chir-r-r-r." This is the call of the red squirrel, enraged at some intruder entering its territory—probably you. If you look about, you will probably see this small, rusty colored squirrel perched on a branch, stamping its feet and jerking its bushy tail back and forth.

Like the chickadees and nuthatches, the red squirrel eats the small, winged seeds of the hemlock. To reach these seeds, the red squirrel shucks the scales off the pendant brown cones, often leaving large piles of scales on a fallen log or stump. You may come across one of these squirrel middens along the trail.

As an isolated island of northern woods, Tillman Ravine harbors a variety of interesting birds more commonly found in Vermont and New Hampshire. A large variety of warblers—small, colorful, insectivorous birds—nest here in Tillman Ravine and other hemlock woods in north-western New Jersey, while they rarely nest elsewhere in New Jersey. Among them are the magnolia, black-throated blue, black-throated green, Canada, and blackburnian warblers and the northern water thrush. The solitary vireo, another bird more commonly found north of here, also nests in Tillman Ravine.

A little further on, the trail flattens out a little, and deciduous woods appear on the right; the white, red, and chestnut oaks remind us that we are still in New Jersey. As you continue, many signs of man's activity become apparent. The trail passes a wall of cobbled sandstone and then a stand of red cedars, both indications that this was once farmland.

As you cross over the wall to follow the brook again, notice the large sugar maple directly across the brook. If you cross the brook at this point (in times of high water this is not always possible), and follow the footpath, you will see just how close to the agricultural past you are. The open farmland spreading out in front of you here is a welcome sight after the closed canopy of the hemlock forest.

Back on the trail, more plants of deciduous woods are seen, such as blueberry, asters, Solomon's seal, and wintergreen. There continue to be signs of disturbance, however. An aspen grove and a gray birch stand suggest a recently abandoned field, as do the stone walls. When you begin to see another pine plantation like the one at the head of the trail, look carefully along the trail. The shiny, black objects you see are pieces of charcoal, and if you look closely, you can see the ruins of an old charcoal kiln to the left of the trail just before it meets the road.

The trail ends at an asphalt road, and from the bridge here, one can watch Tillman Brook flow west to Big Flat Brook, which eventually spills into the Delaware River.

The trail you've just taken is so inviting, you may want to retrace your steps on the return trip, or you can explore one of the side trails that lead away from the brook in the vicinity of Lower Falls.

# 3. Delaware Water Gap National Recreation Area

*Mount Tammany*
Distance: 3½ miles (Difficult)
Walking time: 2–3 hours
Directions: Take Interstate 80 west to the last exit before the New Jersey–Pennsylvania bridge. Follow signs to visitor's center, then follow signs to the rest area (turn left under I-80, then right at stop sign).

---

Ever since the early nineteenth century, the Delaware Water Gap has attracted visitors from all over the world. Some of the earliest visitors were American landscape painters who came to paint this awesome natural wonder. Later, in 1829, the first summer resort, Kittatinny House, was built in the gap. Well-to-do vacationers would come and spend the entire summer enjoying the scenic beauty, outdoor activities, amusement parks, and dance halls of the area. By the turn of the century, transportation to the gap was better and cheaper, and many people could afford to vacation there. Dozens of resort hotels were built, and these served thousands of summer visitors.

Improved roads and air travel eventually provided people with a greater choice of vacation areas, and the resort business declined as summer-long stays were replaced by weekend excursions. The natural beauty that first attracted so many people remains, however, and in 1965 Congress authorized the Delaware Water Gap National Recreation Area to preserve the beauty of the gap and the surrounding area of the Kittatinny Ridge.

The red-dot Mount Tammany trail leaves the parking area near the rear corner of the lot. Its immediate steep ascent should be heeded as a warning of what lies ahead; sturdy boots are a must for this walk. The trail climbs

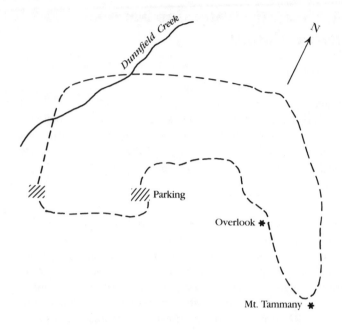

through woods of yellow birch and sugar maple, passing
occasional large hemlocks, and then skirts an outcropping
of reddish rock. This is red sandstone, the principal rock
of this section of the Kittatinny Ridge. As the rivers of this
region carved valleys in the softer red shale rock, ridges
of erosion-resistant sandstone were left.

The trail then passes a slope covered with jumbled
rock. Such an area is called a talus slope, a steep slope
covered by fragments of rock from the top of the hill. Few
plants or animals find this a hospitable environment, but
there is one interesting animal who often makes his home
here: the eastern wood rat. The wood rat looks much like
the Norway rat, but can be distinguished by its longer,
hairier tail, and larger ears, eyes, and whiskers. Although it
is rare to see the wood rat, one can often find piles of

debris and droppings near its nest, which is made in crevices among the talus.

If you are lucky, you may find a wood rat midden, which is composed of various plant materials and an assortment of strange objects. Bottle caps, nails, coins, shotgun shells, watches, keys, and other shiny metal objects are often present, along with bits of paper, rags, rubber bands, and just about anything else the animal can find. This habit of packing off such objects has earned the animal the name pack rat.

The trail becomes steeper and passes scattered rhododendron and mountain laurel. Look carefully for a double red blaze noting a turn to the right; be careful not to continue straight, where someone has marked a series of trees with red paint. As soon as the trail turns, you cut across an exposed section of sandstone beds. The woods here are primarily of chestnut oak, the same ridge-top tree that grows at High Point and all along the Kittatinny Ridge.

Continue to where the trail bends left; there is an overlook here which gives a fine view of Mount Tammany, Mount Minsi (the western flank of the gap), the Delaware River, and Arrow Island below. Beyond lies the broad expanse of the Kittatinny Valley. Looking across to the base of Mount Minsi, you can see how the underlying bedrock appears to have large folds in it. These folds were caused millions of years ago, when pressures from beneath the earth contorted the bedrock into a series of great arches and troughs. In these folds lies the story of how the Delaware Water Gap was formed.

The great arches of that original landscape were huge mountains. These mountains were worn down over millions of years until this area was actually a broad flat plain lying almost at sea level. Then this plain was elevated slightly, and the rivers began to cut deeper into the land. As they did, they caused broad valleys to form in the weaker rock, leaving the erosion-resistant rock as the Kittatinny Ridge. The Delaware River cut through the ridge at the same pace as its tributaries formed the adjoining valleys, resulting in the creation of the gap.

The trail continues along a ridge and passes over more exposed red sandstone. Here the rock has been polished by the great ice sheet that once covered the Kittatinny Ridge. To the left is a flat expanse of low-bush blueberry topped by chestnut oak, hickories, and occasional pitch pine. The blackened trunks of many of the trees indicate that this area has experienced a fire recently. In fall these woods are brilliant with the scarlet of blueberry and the yellow hues of dying grasses.

After cutting across a rocky talus slope, the trail comes to a steep ledge. Though the fracturing pattern of the rock makes for good natural steps, a little rock climbing is required here. Tall hemlocks surround you as you scramble from rock to rock. It is along this part of the trail that you may catch a glimpse of another of the region's more curious mammals: the porcupine.

Occasionally, porcupines are seen waddling casually along the trail, though not commonly, since they are primarily nocturnal. If you do see a porcupine, you may be surprised at how close you can approach it; this is because porcupines are myopic. Stamp your foot, however, and the porcupine is likely to look about and bristle its quills, as he hears well and reacts quickly to touch.

As the trail nears the summit of Mount Tammany, it passes through another section of woods that have been recently swept by fire. At the summit, the trail bears left; continue another ⅛ mile to reach an overlook. If you are walking the trail in spring or fall, by now you have probably heard flocks of Canada geese calling as they flew by high overhead. Spend a while at this overlook, and you are sure to see a few of these flocks. Huge flocks of blackbirds can usually be seen also, and in spring a wide variety of colorful songbirds. All of this avian activity is due to the fact that the Delaware River Valley lies along the Atlantic flyway—the great invisible highway traveled twice each year by millions of birds on their way to and from South and Central America.

In autumn, you may take time here to witness the migration of the diurnal birds of prey, particularly broad-winged and red-tailed hawks. With binoculars, you can watch them as they appear as small specks in the northern sky, growing larger as they rapidly approach, then gliding by you along the ridge to the south.

For the hawks, the Kittatinny Ridge is an extremely important geographical feature. This is because westerly winds striking the flanks of the ridge produce strong updrafts that allow the hawks to soar effortlessly when conditions are right.

The view here is unobscured partly because of the type of vegetation growing: scrub oak. The scrub oak's growth is inhibited in this windy, icy spot, and so it only forms a low shrublike thicket. When back on the trail again, note that the blaze is now light blue. This trail travels along the ridge for a short distance, allowing occasional glimpses of Jenny Jump and Allamuchy Mountains with the Great (Kittatinny) Valley in between. The trail soon swings to the left and begins to descend the ridge along a steep, rocky trail. Before long, the woods change to sugar maple and yellow birch. Below the canopy of these trees grows a layer of smaller trees; this layer is known as the understory. In spring, the most conspicuous understory tree here is the flowering dogwood, its blossoms forming a lovely pink and white layer within the forest. In autumn, witch hazel becomes most obvious, as its scraggly yellow flowers appear in October and November.

At other times of the year, witch hazel can be recognized by its wavy-edged leaves with uneven bases, and its stubby four-part seed pods. The leaves give the plant part of its name: although it is not related to the European hazelnut, the early settlers thought its leaves resembled those of the hazel of their native land. The "witch" part of the name comes from the fact that witches rode on brooms made from the witch hazel. The early settlers used an extract from the witch hazel bark as a remedy for bruises and sprains, and made divining rods from its branches.

The trail flattens out for a short distance, giving one's legs a brief respite, then continues as a steep and rocky path for about ¾ mile. Here it joins the Dunnfield Creek Trail. Shortly, the trail crosses the creek via a footbridge. Dunnfield Creek drops over 1,000 feet from Mount Tammany to the Delaware River, much of it in small waterfalls like the one above the footbridge. The upper part of the creek is flanked by a steep ravine shrouded with tall hemlocks, mountain laurel, and lush growths of fern on the rock outcrops.

In another ¼ mile, a second trail joins from the right; this white-blazed trail is the Appalachian Trail, the famous 2,000-mile trail which goes from Mount Springer in Georgia to Mount Katahdin in Maine. Continue on the white-blazed trail, which follows high above the creek. The hemlocks are joined by American beech and yellow birch trees, with occasional large tulip trees sending their straight-as-an-arrow trunks up out of the very bottom of the ravine. Another tree that grows along here may catch your eye: the American basswood or linden tree. This tree has large heart-shaped, fine-toothed leaves. Its fragrant yellow flowers appear in early summer.

A series of pools, potholes, flumes, and waterfalls characterizes Dunnfield Creek along here as it hurries to meet the Delaware. Many of these pools are visited by trout fishermen, as this is one of the few streams in the state that supports native brook trout. The trail crosses the creek once more and leaves it behind to emerge at the Dunnfield Area parking lot. At the end of the lot, turn left to follow the road back to your car.

# The Highlands

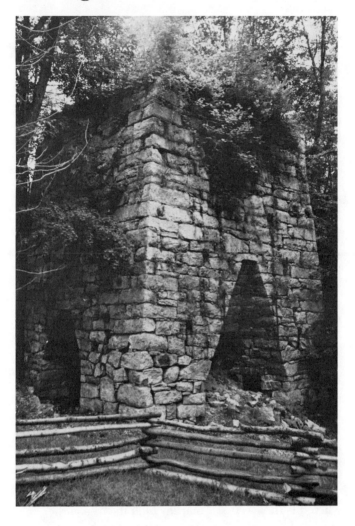

Ruins of old charcoal iron furnace, Wawayanda State Park

# 4. Wawayanda State Park

*Cedar Swamp Trail*
Distance: 5 miles (Moderate)
Walking time: 2½ hours
Directions: Take NJ 23 to Canistear Rd. Go north on
Canistear until it ends. Turn right onto Wawayanda Rd.
and follow to park entrance. Stop at park entrance office
(trailer just beyond the road onto the main parking area)
for trail maps, if desired. Enter the day use area and follow
road to boathouse parking lot. There is a parking fee of
$1.00 on weekdays and $3.00 on weekends. Tuesdays are
free.

Here in Wawayanda State Park, close to the throngs of
civilization, are found the elements of wilderness: black
bear, beaver, bobcat, and wild turkey roam the cedar
swamps, mature forests, and rhododendron jungles of this
area. Because of its unique plant and animal life, portions
of the 6,000-acre park (including the Cedar Swamp Trail)
have recently been designated as natural areas under the
New Jersey Natural Systems Act.

"Wa-wa-yanda" is a phonetic version of a Lenape Indian
word meaning "water on the mountain." The mountain is
one of the broad gneissic ridges that make up the Highlands section of New Jersey, and the water is the beautiful
255-acre Wawayanda Lake. The lake was formerly known
as Double Pond, being two bodies of water separated by a
narrow strip of dry land. This strip can be seen today at
the center of the lake on the west side of Barker Island.
The two ponds became one in the middle of the 1800s
when the Thomas Iron Company built the dam at the
northeastern end of the lake to provide water power for
its iron operations.

This walk begins at the dam. Leave the parking lot on

the gravel road to the left and walk ¼ mile to the dam. After crossing the dam, bear left onto the dirt road and follow this path until you come upon an intersection. To your left are the well-preserved remains of a charcoal blast furnace where iron was produced during the late 1800s. The forty-two-foot-high furnace was built by Oliver Ames and his sons in 1845–1846. One of the sons, William, supervised the construction of the furnace, and his initials W.L.A. and the date 1846 are still visible on the iron lintel in the main arch of the furnace.

Iron ore from the nearby Waywayanda mine (2½ miles to the northeast) was hauled by mules to this site along the road above the furnace. The massive stone wall just behind this road is the foundation of the wooden bridge that spanned the road, allowing the ore to be hauled to the opening at the top of the furnace. From here it was dumped into an iron vat at the bottom of the furnace, whose charcoal-fueled fires reached temperatures of 2,000°F. Pieces of charcoal can be seen scattered along the ground in this area.

The finished iron, in the form of rectangular "pigs," was hauled by mules to Warwick, New York, where it was shipped by railroad to the foundry. The iron from this furnace was used predominantly for casting wheels for railroad cars.

To the right of the furnace can be seen a stone-lined trench or sluiceway. Water was diverted from the creek on the right into this sluiceway to power an eight-foot-long bellows. The bellows supplied oxygen to the roaring fires of the blast furnace. Some of the firebrick which had to withstand the heat of these fires can be seen at the bottom of the main chimney.

In the woods to the right of the furnace was once the village of Double Pond, which grew up around the iron-smelting activity. At one time about 800 people lived here, and the village contained a post office, general store, creamery, blacksmith shop, cheese factory, and saloon. After the furnace closed in 1862, the village gradually died. Today, the woods hide the remains of Double Pond's heyday. Occasionally artifacts are found that serve as reminders of the life that went on here: old cannonballs, a sled from the Thomas Iron Company, and an ice cutter from the days when Double Pond supplied the village with ice.

Head back toward the barn and over the wooden bridge toward the left. This barn once housed the mules used to haul iron to and from the furnace. Now the barn is home for dozens of barn swallows, which in summer can be seen darting through the window to feed their young inside. Just beyond the bridge to the left is a marker saying Double Pond Trail; stay on this trail through the group camping area, and beyond a gate. Here you enter woods of American beech, sugar maple, and yellow birch. On the left, hemlocks squeeze their way through fractures in an impressive outcropping of gneiss.

Continue about ⅓ mile, where the dirt road crosses over a wooden bridge. In summer, the pickerelweed and yellow pond lilies in flower make this a pretty spot. Scattered red maple snags dotted with woodpecker holes can be seen in the wet meadow on either side of the bridge. After the bridge, continue on this path, passing the red-dot trail on the right.

Soon the trail passes through a small cedar swamp, and then about 100 yards further, Cedar Swamp Trail begins at the right. Take this trail, which is still more of a jeep trail than a footpath, until you come to a grove of striped maple. The trail becomes wet here, but look carefully at the muddy spots as you step over them. Deer, raccoon, and bear tracks abound. The bear tracks are unmistakable: about 3½ inches wide by 7 inches long. The slightly smaller tracks you may see are made by the bear's front foot, since often the round heelpad does not leave an imprint. Don't be alarmed; the largely nocturnal black bears in this area are not used to humans and will avoid encounters with them.

Listen closely here to the sound of the wind moving through the tops of the trees, which rise out of the sphagnum-moss-covered hummocks. These are Atlantic white cedar trees, somewhat out of place here, as they are usually found along the coast at much lower elevations. Man has exploited the Atlantic white cedar ever since he came to this area. The light, durable lumber was used in shipbuilding and for shingles and clapboards. During the American Revolution, white cedar charcoal was used in making gunpowder. These and other uses have had a severe impact on the white cedar forests. At present, less than 50,000 acres of cedar woods remain in New Jersey.

Mule barn, Wawayanda State Park

As you continue, look for pickerel frogs jumping between the rushes and horsetails on the trail here. Off to the side of the trail, the red fruits of the wild calla or water arum add color in the late summer, and the smell of sweet pepperbush fills the air.

The trail dries out as you leave the cedar swamp and is immediately engulfed by a dense clump of rhododendron. After the trail emerges into a clearing of ferns, it swings to the right back into rhododendron so thick that you must stoop a little as you walk. In July, the glossy leaves of the rhododendron are a backdrop for the beautiful pink and purple flowers.

Continue along until the trail drops down to a flat with an intermittent stream passing through it. Be careful not to lose the trail here; look for where the stream bed enters the woods. (The blue arrow that points to this spot is sometimes obscured in summer.) After passing through more rhododendron, the trail enters a birch-beech-maple woods that is dotted with rock outcrops. Shortly, the trail comes to a T. Bear left and continue less than ¼ mile to another intersection (Banker Trail) and bear left again. Look for beechdrops along this trail. This parasitic plant lacks any green pigment and is only found in association with American beech trees. Also along the ground in late summer, you'll find the shaggy husks of fallen beechnuts. These nuts provide food for ruffed grouse, raccoons, foxes, deer, squirrels, and chipmunks. Wild turkey, which were reintroduced to this area in 1970, are especially fond of beechnuts.

Where the trail comes upon another Banker Trail marker, bear left. As the trail gradually descends, different trees appear: tulip trees, sassafras, and aspen. At the junction with a yellow-blazed trail, bear left, and continue to where the trail emerges into a clearing with a small pond. Stay to the left of the pond and follow the path into some pine woods. The trail appears to end abruptly at an asphalt road. Turn left onto the dirt road. Go ¼ mile, passing a few houses (the trail has left park property here), and reenter the park where the trail passes between two white posts. This is the trail you began on, the Double Pond Trail, which will take you back to the start.

# 5. Skylands Botanical Gardens

Distance 1¼ miles (Easy)
Walking time: 40 minutes
Directions: Take County Rd. 511 to Shepherd Lake Rd. Go
2½ miles and turn left at the Skylands Manor sign. The
gardens are open April to September. There is a parking
fee of $1.00 on weekdays and $2.00 on weekends.
Admission is free on Tuesdays.

The Skylands section of Ringwood State Park is known
more for the Skylands Manor than for the extensive botan-
ical gardens that surround it. The manor is an elegant
Jacobean mansion which was built in the 1920s for Clarence Mackenzie Lewis. The finest European and American
craftsmen cut its stone and carved its elaborate wood
trim, and inside can be found sixteenth-century stained
glass windows, fireplaces, and paneling from castles and
mansions of Europe. A good way to begin your walk is
to join one of the manor tours, which are conducted
throughout the summer.

Plants were Lewis's hobby, and the gardens are as fascinating as the house. Terraced gardens, a cactus garden,
a wildflower garden, and many other formal and natural
gardens are all arranged here on a 250-acre plateau amid
the Ramapo Mountains.

Begin your walk in the annual garden, across the street
from the manor. Mums, snapdragons, and marigolds burst
with color, joined by a variety of other flowers: alyssum,
coleus, verbena, and begonias, to name a few. The many
nectar-producing flowers attract a beautiful array of butterflies: monarchs, spicebush swallowtails, tiger swallowtails, and others. The annual garden is best visited
after the beginning of June, but remains colorful up until
the first autumn frost.

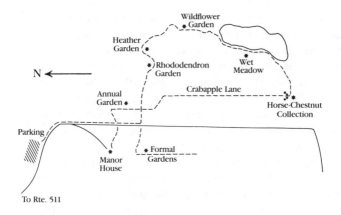

Take the left-hand pathway out of the annual garden to the perennial garden. Some of the plants here may look familiar, since many of them are typical meadow plants: goldenrod, black-eyed Susans, and wild bergamot. In August, the blue and white blossoms of the chaste tree and butterfly bush are numerous.

From the perennial garden, walk to the left and enter the "vista": a lane of crabapple trees imported from China. In early May, this lane is a photographer's delight. From the lawn here can be seen the Ramapo Mountains, where on hot August days it is not uncommon to see turkey vultures gliding over the trees, or red-tailed hawks turning lazy circles above the hills.

Continue down the lane until you reach *The Four Seasons*, a group of four statues depicting figures dressed in spring, summer, fall, and winter dress. Beyond the statues is the horse-chestnut collection. Horse chestnut trees, not native to this area, have long been used in shade-tree plantings because of their interesting leaves and fruit. Most characteristic of these trees are their seven to nine wedge-shaped toothed leaflets and their large, spiny fruits.

There are several other trees in this section of woods that have interesting leaves and fruits. The star-shaped leaves and long-stemmed, prickly fruits that look like a medieval knight's mace belong to the sweet gum tree. The tree gets its name from the sap that exudes from the wounds, and this hardened sap, or gum, is chewed by some people. The straight, tall tree with the peculiar four-pointed leaves is the tulip tree, also known as the yellow or tulip poplar. This tree gets its name from the large tuliplike orange and green flowers which can be seen in May and June. Its fruits are born in upright conelike structures which often remain on the tree throughout the winter. These seeds are eaten by squirrels and a number of birds. The wood of the tulip tree is soft and straight-grained and thus easily worked. In the past, Indians turned the trunks of tulip trees into dugout canoes, while today the wood is used for making furniture, tools, and toys.

The large nuts that you may see along the ground here come from the pignut hickory tree. This tree has compound leaves bearing five leaflets which turn bright yellow in October. The large nuts are eaten by squirrels, chipmunks, and deer mice, and it is possible to tell who has been eating the nuts by the way they've been opened. If you find a nut cut into many pieces, this is the work of a gray squirrel or chipmunk. If the nut has one smooth elliptic opening, however, you have found the work of the flying squirrel, which is rarely seen because of its nocturnal habits. Deer mice open the nuts from two sides.

These three trees—the sweet gum, tulip tree, and pignut hickory—are trees of the southern forest; that is, they are toward the northern end of their range here. In this same small section of woods are also trees more representative of the northern woods. Sugar maple can be recognized by its dark brown bark marked with vertical grooves and ridges and five-lobed leaves. This tree is as valuable for its lumber as it is for its sap, which is collected to make maple syrup. Another northern tree seen here is the larch or tamarack, which is the only northern

Gatehouse, Skylands Manor

conifer that sheds its needles in autumn. Two other conifers, red and white pine, also grow here. The two are
easily distinguished by both their bark and their needles.
The bark of the red pine is reddish and scaly, while that of
the white pine is dark with deep furrows. White pine has
needles in clusters of five, red pine, of two.

Pass by a group of red pines and follow a grassy lane to
Swan Pond. The small, man-made pond is dotted with
fragrant water lilies and bullhead lilies in summer. Forget-
me-nots grow along the edge of the pond among the grass
and reeds. A closer look here will reveal the discarded
exoskeletons of dragonflies and damselflies, which can be
seen darting above the water. These are left behind after
the aquatic nymphs leave the water and emerge via partially submerged plants as winged adults.

On the other side of the pond are a small clump of

rhododendron and one of weeping birch trees. These trees are often used as perches by kingbirds, which sally out over the water to snatch up insects. Growing along the near side of the pond are alders and willows, both typical of wet areas like this. The tall plant with whorled leaves and the domed cluster of pinkish flowers that grows along the path here is spotted joe-pye weed. The wet meadow harbors several other plants that prefer moist soil: sensitive fern, marsh fern, and various orchids. At the end of the pond, the trail becomes quite mucky. Watch your step!

Proceed to where the trail splits and take the right-hand fork, which loops around toward a small creek. Take a left before the stone bridge and enter the wildflower garden. In June, the fragrance of sweet bay magnolia fills the air here, giving way to the aroma of sweet pepperbush in July and August. An incredible variety of native wild-flowers and ferns has been assembled in this garden, and the identification labels on each of the plants make this an excellent place to become familiar with native plants.

Many of the plants growing together here would not be found growing together in the wild. While Indian pipe and rattlesnake plantain orchids are found in woods all through the northeast, bunchberry, another plant growing here in the wildflower garden, only grows in the far north or in the mountains further south. Some of the plants growing together here have widely different soil acidity requirements. Many among them—wintergreen, pink lady's slipper, Canada mayflower, partridgeberry, and Indian cucumber root, for example—prefer quite acidic soil. A few others grow only in sweet soil, soil that is neutral or basic. Dutchman's-breeches, columbine, and some of the ferns—maidenhair, spleenworts, and purple cliffbrake—prefer such conditions.

At the end of the wildflower garden is a wet area of ferns and cattails. Bear right, then left along the pond. This pond, which abounds with frogs and muskrat, is surrounded by sweet pepperbush, Saint-John's-wort, buttonbush, and rose of Sharon, all of which bloom in late summer. In early spring, even before the leaves are out, the drooping white flowers of the shadbush are seen here. This shrub gets its name from the fact that its flowers appear when the shad move up coastal streams to spawn.

Past the pond on the right is a plant with huge leaves. This is a Chilean rhubarb, *Gunnera*, related to the rhubarb grown in home gardens. Beyond this is the "moraine garden," which contains plants that thrive under the hot, dry surface conditions typical of talus slopes and rocky areas in alpine regions. These plants have roots that grow deep to tap water well below the surface. Here in the garden, this condition is recreated by burying concrete water tanks which can be replenished. Most of the plants growing here are heathers: their tiny leaves and prostrate growth habit are typical of alpine plants. The heathers grown here are from all over Europe: England, France, Belgium, and the Netherlands.

The next stop, the rhododendron garden, should be visited in June when the many-colored rhododendron blossoms are joined by azalea and mountain laurel flowers. From here, walk through the perennial garden and across the road to the magnolia walk, which is especially beautiful in June. Next, pass through the summer garden, which is filled with a variety of flowers. As you walk through, see if you can guess how each flower gets its name—bee balm, wormwood, beardtongue, alum root, bellflower, tickseed, and mistflower.

As you finish your walk at the peony garden and return to your car, try to picture the gardens in the era when Clarence Mackenzie Lewis had scores of gardeners maintaining the grounds. Today, the state must make do with a very small staff, assisted by volunteers from the Skylands Association.

# 6. Ramapo Mountain State Forest

*Ramapo Lake*
Distance: 4½ miles (Difficult)
Walking time: 3 hours
Directions: From the north, take NJ 208 north to end
(Oakland). From the south, take NJ 23 to US 202 north,
and go 7 miles to W. Oakland Ave. Continue on W.
Oakland Ave., then turn right onto Skyline Drive. Go 1¼
miles to Camp Tamarack Boy Scout Camp (on right). The
parking lot for Ramapo Mountain State Forest is directly
across the street.

---

Just before you begin to ascend Skyline Drive, you cross
the scenic Ramapo River; in one sense, this walk begins
there. The Ramapo (an Indian name meaning "formed of
round ponds") flows along the Great Border Fault, where
200 million years ago the earth's crust to the west of the
fault was uplifted. The mountains that were formed have
been greatly eroded since then, producing the Highlands,
a range of ridges and plateaus of which the Ramapo
Mountains are a part.

The rocks of the Highlands are truly ancient. Some 1.2
*billion* years ago, these rocks had their beginnings as
sediments being deposited in a vast undersea basin.
Mudstone and shale were gradually formed from these
sediments, then later subjected to ages of intense heat and
pressure, producing the extremely hard rock called
gneiss. This ancient rock can be seen exposed at many
places along this walk.

From the parking lot, walk past the gate and follow the
asphalt road to a sign that says Foot Trail—Ramapo Lake.
The trail begins as a wide, level path, but be advised that
it becomes much more difficult later on; sturdy shoes are
strongly recommended.

Almost immediately after you enter the trail, there is a large outcrop of gneiss on the right. If you are carrying a compass, hold it up to a section of this rock and see what happens. If the needle spins out of its normal position, you've found a deposit of iron ore, or magnetite. These deposits are found throughout the Ramapo Mountains and are believed to have been introduced into the surrounding metamorphic rock during volcanic activity deep below the surface. In addition, iron oxide deposits are found locally; these are produced by weathering of the magnetite. These deposits were mined from the beginning of the 1700s until quite recently, although maximum production was reached around 1880.

This and later sections of the trail are part of the old Cannonball Road, along which lie many old iron mines; some of the roads that served these mines became part of a road used by the Continental Army during the Revolutionary War to transport munitions—hence the name Cannonball Road. This mountainous route afforded safety from British attacks on vital supplies of weapons and ammunition.

Continue along the trail, bearing right at a fork that leads downhill. Just before the trail joins a paved road, bear left. The trail passes some downed trees and then goes under a large red oak that has two trees lying on top of it. All of these downed trees give evidence that you are walking along a ridge top: the trees here are exposed to the winds and are toppled more frequently than those growing on the protected slopes below.

Many of these windblown trees have been worked by pileated woodpeckers, whose large, characteristically rectangular excavations in search of carpenter ants can be seen in some of the dead trees lying along the trail. Although the pileated woodpecker is not often seen, its relative the common flicker is frequently seen searching the ground for ants and beetle larvae. Its loud "wicker" call, golden wing linings, and white rump patch make the flicker unmistakable.

The trail passes a number of large tulip trees, and then along a small ravine flanked by ferns. Shortly it crosses over a grass-covered stone bridge and through an area of jumbled fractured rock.

The minerals that make up the gneiss in these rock outcrops are arranged in parallel layers, and as the rock weathers, it tends to break up along these layers into angular blocks. A strikingly different type of rock, which is speckled with white pebbles, can be seen occasionally along the trail here. This is Green Pond formation conglomerate, made up of hard reddish purple sedimentary rock containing pebbles of white quartz. If you were to look for the source of this rock, you would have to look some ten miles to the northwest, to Schunemunk Mountain. The pieces of conglomerate rock in the Ramapo Mountains were plucked from Schunemunk Mountain more than 10,000 years ago, then carried by the ice to their resting place here. Such glacially transported rocks are known as erratics, since they are dramatically different from the underlying rock.

The trail passes out into a small clearing ringed by stunted chestnut oaks. The chestnut oak is most easily identified by its leaves, which have seven to seventeen pairs of rounded teeth, and its dark, deeply ridged bark. The chestnut oak survives better than most trees on the thin, dry soils of the northern New Jersey ridgetops, and is thus characteristic of the upland forest along these mountains.

Underneath the chestnut oaks here, and in most places where it is the dominant tree, very few shrubs or wild-flowers grow. The acid-loving heath shrubs such as blueberry, huckleberry, and mountain laurel are found, while bracken fern, goldenrod, and asters are the most commonly seen herbaceous plants. Before passing out of this clearing, look up, as this is a good spot to view hawks or turkey vultures flying overhead.

The trail continues through a thicket of mountain laurel, past an interesting rock outcrop, and then emerges onto a paved road. Bear left here and go down the hill until you reach the dam. This dam was built by a group of sportsmen who bought the area to create a lake for fishing. At that time, the area was known as Rotten Pond. This name came indirectly from the Dutch settlers who first lived here, who called it "rote" (rat) pond. The "rats" were muskrat which they trapped here. Today, Rotten Pond is Ramapo Lake, a peaceful mountain fishing spot.

Before the dam, bear right and follow the road which

Gneiss outcrop, Ramapo Mountain State Forest

goes around the lake. The ruins of a large stone building known as The Castle can be seen on a nearby hill. Built in 1910, the building was destroyed by fire in 1962.

Continue to a fork in the road and bear left. The road soon passes the ranger station and then forks again; bear left again. A short detour to the left along any part of this section of the road gives an excellent view of the southern end of the lake. This end is very shallow, and during dry periods, old tree stumps can be seen sticking above the water. Great blue herons, green herons, wood ducks, and mallards can usually be seen feeding among the purple-flowered loosestrife and pond lilies along the edge of the lake here.

Return to the road and pass a grassy path that leads to the right. About 100 yards further, the road forks again. Bear right onto a broken-up asphalt road. Just as this road makes a horseshoe bend downhill, look for a yellow-blazed trail on the left. Follow this trail as it descends sharply toward a creek. Cross the creek and then scramble alongside of an outcrop. There are both yellow and red trail markers on this section of the trail.

The trail emerges onto the first of a series of overlooks. The town of Oakland is to the left. Crystal Lake is below, and in the distance to the right, the northernmost portion of the First Watchung Mountain.

Follow the yellow-blazed trail which skirts a ledge, and as the trail goes up over more rock, look back to see the long, narrow form of Lake Inez. A short distance further, the trail comes to a small stand of pitch pine and scrub oak. These two trees replace the chestnut oak on a very few ridge tops in the state, where they must withstand not only thin, dry soil, but severe climatic conditions. Strong winds, frequent sleet and ice storms, and periodic fires make this a tough spot for any tree to grow. Note how the pitch pine clings to the rock.

A few chickadees may be seen on these ridge tops but little else in the way of bird life. Dense foliage and water are a requirement for most birds, and neither of these requirements is met on these dry, sparse ridge tops.

The trail leads to another outcrop, with good views to the west toward the Wyanokie Plateau. From here, cross over the back of the rock and reenter the woods. The trail forks—take the red trail to the right—and then comes to another fork in ⅓ mile. Bear right and follow the trail a short distance to the final overlook. Pale corydalis, a relative of wild bleeding heart, grows on this outcrop.

Retrace your steps to the fork and bear right. You may notice that the trees are slightly different along the trail here, and that it is generally cooler and wetter than on the previous section of the trail. This is a north-facing slope, and as such is protected from the sun's dessicating rays. The relatively moist conditions that prevail here support a greater variety of trees, shrubs, and wildflowers.

The trail continues down the hill to an even moister

area; the reed grass, ferns, witch hazel, and even skunk cabbage seem a welcome relief after the dry sparseness of the ridge tops.

A short way further, the trail comes out at the dam. From here, follow the road back to the parking lot.

# 7. Waterloo Village

Distance: 1½ miles (Easy)
Walking time: 3 hours
Directions: Take Interstate 80 to exit 25 in Stanhope. Go
north 4 miles on US 206 and follow signs to Waterloo
Village. The village is open from the Tuesday after Easter
through December, Tuesday to Sunday from 10:00 A.M. to
6:00 P.M. There is a fee of $3.50 for adults, $2.50 for
senior citizens, and $1.75 for children 6–12 years old.

Once described as "the only first-class ghost town in the
northeastern United States," Waterloo Village is coming to
life again as a living museum of New Jersey's past. This
walk through the restored village and along the towpath
of the Morris Canal takes you through more than a century of fascinating American history. The walk gives one a
sense of the forces that change people's relations with the
land, and with each other.

Although some of the buildings within the village are
closed to the public, the majority are open, and are staffed
with interpreters who can describe in detail the activities
associated with their particular building. It is suggested,
however, that one begin or end with this walking tour to
help fit together the pieces of this historical jigsaw puzzle.

From the parking area, walk past the concert area to
the herb garden. Herbs from the garden were put to many
domestic uses; to find out more about these uses, stop at
the next building. Formerly a "gentleman's barn" from
Victorian times, this barn now houses an apothecary shop
and herb-drying rooms. Next, you pass a barn that houses
a carriage collection, and then another barn, which now
houses textile artisans.

At the white barn, turn right and follow the road, which

leads toward the river, and then bear right. The road passes a row of imposing buildings: the Iron Master's house, the Peter Smith house, the Miller's house, and the Stagecoach Club and Tavern. Continue past the Homestead, a stone horse barn which was converted to a home in the early nineteenth century. After the Homestead, the road passes the Wellington house, the Canal house, the Nathan Smith house, and finally the Methodist Church.

At the Methodist Church, turn and retrace your steps, this time following the waterway to your right. This is a section of the Morris Canal, which was the principal reason for the growth and development of the town of Waterloo. The canal, which went from the Delaware River at Phillipsburg to the mouth of the Hudson at Newark, was completed in 1831.

The Morris Canal was largely built to supply fuel to the many iron forges and furnaces located throughout the New Jersey Highlands. The fuel, anthracite coal, could be easily obtained from the Lehigh Valley just across the river from Phillipsburg. The coal was transported in long, narrow barges called canal boats, which were pulled along by mules. These boats carried up to seventy-five tons of cargo, which included grain, wood, bricks, and lumber as well as coal and iron ore. With such heavy loads, the boats traveled at less than two miles per hour, and the complete journey took five days.

The stone building you come to was a general store, built here on the bank of the Morris Canal in 1831. The canal boats could float right up to the store's back door, and the drivers could conduct their business without ever setting foot on land. Many boats went by each day, and the store was a successful business venture for the Smith family, who built many of the homes that you have passed on your walk through the village.

Just past the general store is guard lock 3 of the Morris Canal. This guard lock is actually a combination masonry lock and wooden aqueduct which carried boats over the mill tailrace (to the left) and into the lock pond (at the right). The building to the left of the lock is a blacksmith's shop which records show to have been operating as early as 1790. After 1831, the shop's business boomed, because the canal mules were constantly in need of new shoes.

Follow the wooden bridge across the lock pond to the other side. The cleared path that lies ahead is inclined plane 4 of the Morris Canal, which was recently named a National Historic Engineering Site by the American Society of Civil Engineers. This and the twenty-two other inclined planes along the length of the Morris Canal were built to haul the canal boats up hills that could not be easily circumvented. Via the thirty-four locks and twenty-three inclined planes, a boat traveling between Newark and Phillipsburg was lifted and lowered some 2,134 feet.

How was the seventy-five-ton canal boat moved up this hill, which has a vertical rise of eighty feet? Walk up the plane, and you will notice smooth granite blocks imbedded in the path. These huge stone "sleepers" were the foundation for a boat railway; the holes in the face of the granite blocks are from the rivets that once held the tracks in place. A large wooden plane car or cradle, which held the canal boat, rode along the tracks as the boat

General store at Waterloo Village (Morris Canal in foreground)

slowly made its way up the inclined plane. The canal boat entered the cradle in the lock pond below, as the canal mules were unhitched after crossing over the wooden bridge.

The power for this boat railway came from the canal above the inclined plane. A flume carried water from the canal to a penstock, a long vertical conduit which led to a turbine. The weight of the falling water turned the turbine, which through a series of gears wound a cable around a steel drum twelve feet in diameter. The cable, attached to the plane car, drew the heavy load to the top of the plane. After the plane car reached the top, the boat reentered the canal.

Where the inclined plane path ends, look for a footpath leading to the right of the canal. This is the old towpath, which can be followed for a few hundred yards through the woods.

When the canal was operating, this land was all open farmland. Because so much land had been cleared of timber, firewood was in short supply, and farmers along the canal took advantage of the plentiful supply of coal which floated by each day on the canal boats. Many would barter produce for the coal, but some had craftier methods. A common trick was for a farmer to set up bottles as targets for the canal boatmen, who would throw pieces of coal at them.

After ¼ mile or so, retrace your steps to the inclined plane. The high stone embankments on either side of the wide path are a visible reminder of the force that led to the decline and eventual abandonment of the Morris Canal. A trestle of the Sussex Railroad, which was built in 1854, used to span these embankments. The railroad could carry iron and coal more quickly and cheaply than the canal boats could, and by 1900, the Morris Canal had become obsolete.

Cross over the bridge again and turn right along the water. To the right is the Musconetcong River, and to the left, the millpond of the gristmill and plaster mill. At the far end of the millpond, you pass a grassy mound; this is all that remains of the Andover Forge, which was built in 1763. The forge processed pig iron from Andover Furnace seven miles to the north. By heating the iron and then pounding it with a great iron hammer, which was activated by a waterwheel, the iron was made stronger. The forge's four hammers weighed six hundred pounds each, and the waterwheel that drove them was twenty-five feet in diameter. As was true of many of the forges and furnaces in northern New Jersey, the Andover Forge became an important source of iron and steel for armaments used by the Continental Army during the Revolutionary War.

Continue to the end of the peninsula and cross over to "shore" again. Ahead of you lies a small building which houses the museum of the Canal Society of New Jersey. A visit to the museum makes a good final stop on your walk through Waterloo Village. Here you can see photographs of the canal boats and boatmen, a variety of artifacts associated with canal life, and even a scale model of the inclined plane seen earlier on the walk.

# 8. Scherman and Hoffman Wildlife Sanctuaries

Distance: 2½ miles (Moderate)
Walking time: 1½ hours
Directions: Take Interstate 287 to the Bernardsville exit (from the north), or to the North Maple Ave. West exit (from the south). Proceed to the traffic light at US 202 near the Old Mill Inn. Go straight at this light onto Child's Rd. Continue about 100 yards to a fork and bear right onto Hardscrabble Rd. The parking lot is one mile ahead on the right. The sanctuary trails are open from 9:00 A.M. to 5:00 P.M. every day except holidays.

The Scherman and Hoffman wildlife sanctuaries, operated by the New Jersey Audubon Society, comprise about 250 acres in the southeastern corner of the Highlands. The short, relatively easy trail loop and small nature museum make for a pleasant morning's visit, especially for families.

From the nature museum, follow the red-blazed Dogwood Trail up the rocky slope. On this lower part of the slope grow red, black, and white oaks, red maples, sugar maples, and tall tulip trees. The fast-growing tulip trees, though not most numerous of the species present, seem to dominate the forest on this slope, since they tower over the oaks and maples. However, their seedlings cannot thrive in the shade cast by the growing forest, which if left undisturbed, may come to be dominated by sugar maple, whose seedlings are shade tolerant. Though the mature tulip trees may retain their positions by virtue of a few feet advantage in height, this great height often dooms them, for the brittle wood is susceptible to damage by wind and lightning.

The trail makes a number of switchbacks as it continues up the slope. The angular blocks of gneiss scattered about

55

indicate that you are still in the Highlands, though this area differs from the other walks in the Highlands in that it is south of the area that was covered by the most recent glacial advance, the Wisconsin ice sheet. This makes for subtle differences in the terrain along this walk; there are not the ice-polished outcrops seen in the Ramapo Mountains to the north, and the soil along the ridge here is deeper, not having been scraped away by the glacier.

This trail gets its name from one of the understory trees growing below the forest canopy, the flowering dogwood. This small tree, which rarely exceeds thirty feet in height and eight inches in girth, is one of the first understory trees to appear in the growing forests throughout much of the state. It usually persists as a component of the understory even after the forest has reached the climax stage.

Flowering dogwood is identified by its dark, deeply checkered bark and by its broad, elliptic leaves with five to six pairs of veins. In autumn these leaves turn deep scarlet, thus outlining the understory layer quite distinctly. (Fall is a good time of year to become acquainted with the common trees and shrubs, as their colors allow you to study their distribution from a distance.) Equally distinctive are the flowering dogwood's deceptive "flowers": its showy white petals are actually modified leaves or bracts, and the flowers (more properly called "florets") themselves are clustered at the center. The flowers develop into bunches of red berries in the fall, and these form an important source of food for a variety of animals during the colder months: ruffed grouse, cardinals, evening grosbeaks, and gray squirrels in particular. The dogwood was an important tree to our colonial forefathers also, not for its berries, but for its hard, dense wood. Dogwood was used by them for making tool handles, sled runners, and shuttles for weaving, since its close-grained wood has the quality of becoming smooth with use.

The trail continues up the slope, passing a few American beech trees along the way. The American beech is unmistakable because of its smooth, gray bark. One of these beeches along the right side of the trail has grown up around a large gneiss boulder. There is a space between the tree and the rock where squirrels often cache seeds from nearby beech and tulip trees. Toward the top of the ridge, the trail passes a clump of blackberry bushes. From a crack in a gneiss outcrop near these bushes grows ebony spleenwort, a delicate fern with shining dark stems. While many of the spleenworts prefer shaded areas with sweet (basic) soil, the ebony spleenwort thrives in slightly acidic soil and can even tolerate full sun if there is enough moisture.

The trail passes an old stone wall, a reminder that this ridge was once cleared of its vegetation. Near the wall are a number of bleached and broken American chestnut stumps. The chestnut was once a very common tree with a range that included most of the eastern third of the United States. It was an extremely valuable tree also:

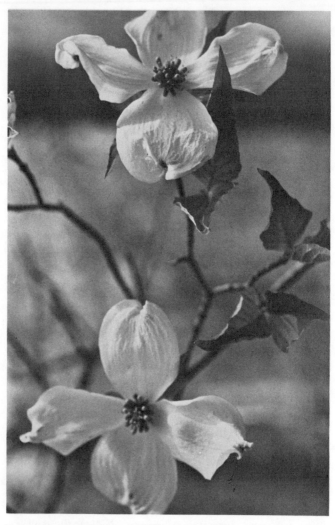

Flowering Dogwood, Scherman Sanctuary

the decay-resistant wood was in great demand for furniture, musical instruments, and railroad ties, and the nuts were both an important wildlife forage and a delicacy for people. In 1890, a fungal blight was accidentally introduced into the country on infected nursery trees brought into New York City from China. From New York the blight spread at a rate of about twenty miles per year, so that by 1920 it had destroyed virtually every chestnut tree in the northeast.

Though no longer a significant component of the northeastern forest, the chestnut has not disappeared completely. Today it survives as an understory tree, sprouting from the roots and stumps of older blight-killed trees. Just as these sprouts reach the point of flowering and fruiting, however, the blight, visible as a ring of orange blisters on the lower trunk, takes hold and quickly kills the tree.

Here toward the top of the ridge, chestnut oak and black birch become more common than on the slopes below. Chestnut oak is the familiar ridge-top tree common throughout the Highlands and along the Kittatinny Ridge. The black birch is easily recognized by the smooth, shiny, almost black bark on younger trees; on older trees the bark becomes scaly and breaks up into plates much like its relative the river birch. The light-colored horizontal markings, called lenticels, serve as pores, allowing gases to pass through the outer bark of the tree. These lenticels become stretched as the tree grows, causing the bark to peel off in some places. (This is more noticeable on white and yellow birch.) Black birch is often called sweet birch, because its twigs contain oil of wintergreen; a mild tea can be made by steeping the young twigs in boiling water.

As you cross the top of the ridge and begin to descend, to the right of the trail there is a distinctive black birch tree which has "merged" with a tulip tree, probably after having been knocked over in a storm. The tulip tree has grown a burl of woody tissue to protect itself from the abrasion caused by the birch trunk, and has sent one of its

*Scherman and Hoffman Sanctuaries* 59

branches skyward to catch more light than its downward-tilted branches can receive.

The struggle for sunlight is evidenced by another plant along the trail here, the wild grape. This familiar vine is commonly found on abandoned agricultural land, since often birds and mammals will drop grape seeds in old fields. This is how these vines began; after being transported to this field and dropped, they germinated and grew until they climbed onto nearby young trees and shrubs. In their vigorous fight to remain in the sunlight, these vines have reached upward with the trees as they grew. The special mechanism that allows the grapevine to do this is its tendrils, slender twining outgrowths of the stem. Another vine growing nearby, which contrasts with the grape in its method of climbing, is poison ivy. It makes its way skyward by means of small aerial rootlets which become attached to the bark of the tree. These rootlets can be readily seen as the dense covering of dark fibers along the poison ivy stem.

The trail passes over another stone wall and continues downhill past some large snags bearing rectangular excavations, suggesting that they have been worked over for carpenter ants by a pileated woodpecker. This side of the hill, facing north, is noticeably cooler than the south side, where the trail began. This partially accounts for the difference in vegetation along this part of the trail: ironwood, a moisture-loving tree that is part of the understory here on the lower portion of the north slope, was not present on the warmer, drier south slope.

Where the trail forks, swing left and follow the trail over the Passaic River. The Passaic is more like a brook here, perhaps less than a mile from its headwaters. From here it travels through the Great Swamp and then flows north until it reaches other branches within the Watchung basin. The Passaic eventually drains through the Second Watchung Mountain at Little Falls, and makes its final escape through the First Watchung Mountain at Great Falls in Paterson.

The trail follows the river through cool woods of beech and yellow birch, the ground carpeted in some places with lush growths of fern. After about ⅓ mile, it crosses the river via a slightly dilapidated footbridge before emerging into an open field. Follow along the edge of the field and then swing right at a wooden fence. After passing a couple of old chicken coops, swing right across the road and follow the trail back into the woods to return to the parking lot.

# The Piedmont

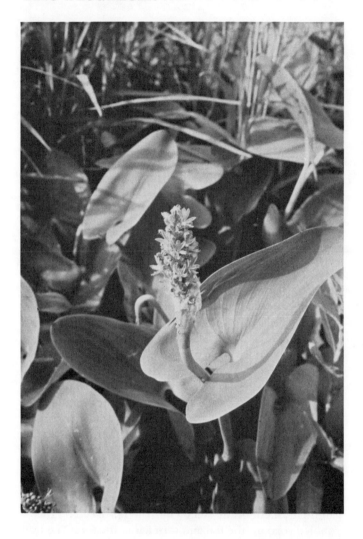

Pickerelweed, Lord Stirling Park

# 9. Palisades Interstate Park

Distance: 5 miles (Difficult)
Walking time: 2½ hours
Directions: Take US 9W to exit 2. Follow road past park headquarters to Alpine picnic area. The parking fee is $1.00.

As you enter the parking lot, notice the reddish sandstone walls along the rear of the lot. Some 190 million years ago, while this sandstone was being formed, molten rock was forced upward through its horizontal layers to form a long, narrow, vertical sill. The softer sandstone has been eroded away, leaving the forty-mile long monolith known as the Palisades, named for its resemblance to a palisaded village. The Indian name for this ridge, Weh-awk-en, describes its appearance equally well; the middle syllable "awk" means "rocks that resemble trees."

Begin your walk at the end of the parking lot, where a gravel path leads past a white house on the left. The house, known as Cornwallis's Headquarters, was a riverside tavern that served riverboat captains and their crews. On November 19, 1776, Lord Cornwallis and some 5,000 British and Hessian soldiers crossed the Hudson from the New York side and scaled the cliffs at Closter Landing in order to surprise Gen. George Washington and his men who were encamped at Fort Lee and Hackensack. It is thought that Lord Cornwallis preceded the troops and paused briefly for food and shelter at this tavern.

Continue a short distance further on the path to a monument marking the place where Cornwallis's men began their ascent of the steep cliff. Then proceed on the cobbled road up the hill and turn left at the fork. The trail ascends through woods of hemlock, sugar maple, tulip trees, and black birch. All but the tulip tree are more typical of northern than southern forests, and they grow here because the ravine affords them a cool, moist refuge from the drier ridge tops above.

The trail here and in many other places is flanked by poison ivy; be careful! Continue past a lovely stone archway and bear right onto the blue-blazed path. Shortly the trail meets the entrance road and follows it past park headquarters, then reenters the woods 100 yards further on the right. The woods along here are predominantly maple with scattered pine, beech, and sweet gum.

Notice how the exposed rock on this section of the trail is quite smooth. This is the result of polishing by fine rock fragments dragged across the Palisades ridge by the Wisconsin glacier. The glacier also carved scratches, known as striations, into the rock along the Palisades ridge, and these can also be seen along this part of the trail.

A short distance further, a side trail leads to the right. Follow this along the edge of a deep, narrow canyon and over a cement bridge to an overlook. You are now standing on the largest section of separated rock in the Palisades: Grey Crag. The crag is some 300 feet long and 10 to 20 feet wide. Here is a good place to view the Palisades up close. The many-sided columns you see were formed by huge vertical fissures in the rock, which were produced as the magma cooled and contracted. Horizontal cracks often intersect these vertical fissures, with the result that the diabase rock tends to break down into distinct masses that resemble stairs. This resemblance has led to calling this and other formations of intruded igneous rock traprock, a term derived from the Swedish "trapp," meaning stairs.

Retrace your steps to the trail and make another detour to the right just before crossing a footbridge to reach another overlook. Hemlocks squeeze their way out of the rock ledge here. In winter, both the hemlocks and the ledge are occasionally draped with snow or ice, the ice sometimes hanging in long columns formed by small cascades.

Continue along over the creek and through a hemlock grove. Partridgeberry, a delicate, evergreen, trailing plant with small heart-shaped leaves, is one of the few plants that can survive the acid soil conditions beneath the hemlocks. Here and elsewhere on the trail it is the most conspicuous herb.

The trail eventually swings to the right over a footbridge built of fractured rock and through an area of gray birch and staghorn sumac. Staghorn sumac is a tall shrub bearing long, compound leaves with eleven to thirty-one sharply toothed leaflets. The young branches and leaf stalks are densely covered with soft hairs, giving them a velvety appearance. The presence of gray birch and staghorn sumac indicates some type of disturbance, and closer inspection will reveal that the area has experienced a fire recently. A side trail leads to a nice overlook, where gulls can often be seen gliding effortlessly above the river. In the fall, if one is lucky, a peregrine falcon may be seen

Cornwallis's headquarters, Palisades Interstate Park

passing these cliffs during its migration south. These magnificent birds formerly nested on ledges along the Palisades, until their near extinction from the effects of pesticides. It is hoped that captive-bred peregrines will someday have eyries here again.

The trail ends abruptly at Ruckman's Point, where there is a small clearing bounded by a concrete wall; the cliff here is 520 feet high. This is one of the many "pitching places" along the Palisades, where wood cut from the ridge-top forest was pitched over the cliff. Below were usually smooth or small-stone talus slopes where the wood would not smash or wedge upon landing. Originally, these forests supplied fuel to the Hudson River steamboats, then later for the home-heating needs of wealthy New Yorkers, who bought up sections of the cliffs for just this purpose.

Follow the grassy path (Ruckman's Road) away from the cliff and then swing right into the woods. The trail passes a series of clefts in the rock. Look carefully along the left for a trail that leads over these clefts. About ½ mile further it reaches the New Jersey State Federation of Women's Clubs Memorial. The federation was instrumental in getting the enabling legislation passed that resulted in the creation of the Palisades Interstate Park Commission in 1900.

The impetus for the creation of such a commission was the destruction of the cliffs by commercial quarrying in the 1800s. The traprock cliffs were blasted to supply ship's ballast in the middle of the century, then later for building material for Manhattan roads and buildings. A large quarry in the Palisades at Haverstraw, New York, still supplies this valuable rock for a variety of commercial uses. One can usually see barges from this quarry bearing the name New York Trap Rock Company being towed along the Hudson River.

The trail reenters the woods behind the monument and continues as a blue-and-white-blazed trail. At a fork, bear right to follow a steep series of steps down to the River Trail. At the bottom, turn left for a short distance and stop just before a stand of white birch trees, which are seldom seen this far south. From here look up to Ruckman's Point (south) and Indian Head to the north. The Indian head formed by the crags looks more like a stoic Yankee settler from this vista.

Retrace your steps past the ascending path and follow the white-blazed shore path. Most of the trees at the base of the talus slopes along here are black locusts, recognized by their delicate compound leaves and thorned branches. Scattered among the locusts are Princess-trees, which were imported from Asia for the old estate gardens along where the Palisades Parkway now lies. The clusters of large purple flowers appear in May.

In about ¾ mile, the trail emerges onto a grassy area known as Twombley's Landing. Oyster shell middens found here indicate that this is the site of a former Indian camp. A quarter of a mile further the trail forks, the right fork leading along the base of the cliff, while the left fork leads along the shore past Excelsior Dock. The trails rejoin and ½ mile further the parking area is reached.

# 10. Great Falls/S.U.M. Historic District

Distance: 2 miles (Easy)
Walking time: 2 hours
Directions: From the east, take Interstate 80 west to the
Paterson Main Street exit, then go left 2 blocks to Grand
St. Turn left and go 4 blocks to Spruce St. From the west,
take the Central Business District exit which loops under
I-80 to Grand St. Turn left and go one block to Spruce St.
Turn right, go 3 blocks to McBride Ave. exit, and turn
right again. Park at Haines Overlook Park, which is
immediately on the left.

Paterson has been called "the cradle of American industry." Here the cotton industry developed the cotton-duck
sail, the locomotive industry produced a significant portion of the nation's locomotives, the world's leading silk-
manufacturing center was founded, the first submarine
was invented, and the Colt revolver and Wright's airplane
engines were manufactured. Most of these early industries
depended on the Great Falls—a 280-foot-wide waterfall
which plunges nearly 80 feet through a narrow gorge—
for their power. Harnessed by a unique group of American entrepreneurs, this inexpensive and abundant source
of energy brought Paterson to national prominence during the nineteenth century.

By the early twentieth century, labor unrest and an
exodus of industry to the south removed Paterson from
the forefront of American industry, but much of the city's
rich engineering, industrial, and architectural heritage can
be seen today in the Great Falls of the Passaic/S.U.M. Historic District.

From the parking lot, you can see the Great Falls
straight ahead, framed by massive cliffs of basalt. This
basalt was formed about 200 million years ago during the

late Triassic period, when large amounts of lava poured out from rifts caused by stress deep beneath the earth's surface. The lava cooled quickly and was later covered by sediments, but was uncovered again when the basin in which Paterson now lies was tilted. This tilting caused rapid erosion of the softer sedimentary rock around the solidified lava, leaving it as a basaltic ridge known as the First Watchung Mountain.

At this particular point along the First Watchung Mountain, the ridge is traversed by the Passaic River, which passes through a narrow gorge that is the result of collapse of the basalt along weak zones in the jointed rock. Huge sections of rock that have fallen away from the cliffs can be seen lying at the base of the falls. (Remember that the falls are most spectacular after a heavy rain.)

Next to the overlook area is a statue of Alexander Hamilton, who first envisioned the falls as a source of power for industry. As secretary of the treasury during the late 1700s, Hamilton tried to involve the government in developing a planned industrial city around the Great

Falls. Congress rejected the idea, but Hamilton succeeded in encouraging a group of prominent businessmen to undertake the planning and operating of such a city. In 1791, the group incorporated as the Society for the Establishment of Useful Manufactures (S.U.M.), a corporation that was to shape Paterson's growth for more than 150 years.

From the overlook, walk back toward McBride Avenue, turn right, and follow the road to the path that leads to the bridge across the Great Falls. (In winter, the gate may be closed, as beautiful but treacherous layers of ice are formed on the bridge.) Below lies the S.U.M. Hydro-electric Generating Plant, man's most recent effort at harnessing the power of the Great Falls. The S.U.M. built the plant in 1914 to produce energy for the mills nearby, its four huge turbines generating 21 million kilowatts per year. Though it has been closed since 1969, the city hopes to reactivate the plant, which could provide thousands of homes and factories with electricity.

After crossing the footbridge, swing left along the edge of the falls. This is a good place to see how the basalt cliff has broken up into a series of narrow chasms. The remains of an early stone dam that crossed the river can be seen from here also. You then pass the Passaic Valley Water Commission and Testing Station and the S.U.M. Conduit House before turning left. This path passes the remains of the S.U.M. Steam Plant, built in 1876, and follows along Maple Street for a short distance.

The path swings left to run parallel to the bank of the pool above the falls and then joins Wayne Avenue. Turn left and follow this road over the river—upstream can be seen the concrete dam built in 1838 to supply water to the S.U.M. raceway—and then turn right onto Spruce Street. Immediately on the right is a gate which opens onto a footpath along the upper raceway; go through this gate and follow the path. The raceway, built between 1828 and 1846, drew water from the Passaic and supplied it to the mills via spillways and wooden flumes. Near the entrance to the raceway on the left can be seen the spill-way that fed the wheelhouse of the Ivanhoe Paper Mill. The wheelhouse, built in 1865, housed an 87-inch turbine that supplied power to a complex of ten buildings where paper was manufactured from rags. These buildings are gone now, but the wheelhouse itself stands and is cur-rently undergoing restoration.

Follow the raceway to the end; here a spillway used to lead down to the middle raceway, which can be seen below. Next to the spillway is a mulberry tree, identified by its heart-shaped, fine-toothed leaves which are often lobed. The mulberry was introduced from Asia in an at-tempt to feed silkworms for the silk industry. The attempt was unsuccessful, however, and Paterson's silk mills were forced to import raw silk from China and Japan.

Retrace your steps along the raceway and turn right onto Spruce Street. Along the right side of the street are a number of large mills. The Barbour Flax Company made linen thread and twine beginning in 1865, while the Dol-phin Jute Company, established in 1844, converted hemp and jute into twine, rope, and carpet backing. One of Paterson's largest mills, the Dolphin Company encom-passed seventeen buildings.

Just past the Dolphin Jute Mill, turn right onto Barbour Street and follow it out to Grand Street. Barbour Street is paved with cobblestone, as once many of Paterson's streets were, and one can easily imagine the sound of carts carrying goods from the mills rolling along this street. At Grand Street turn left and then left again to return to Spruce Street.

Down the street 1½ blocks on the right is the Rogers Locomotive Erecting Shop, built in 1835, and rebuilt in 1871. The eighty-ton locomotives constructed here began as small parts on the top floor and were put together in stages, each larger assembly gradually moving down to-ward the main floor. The completed engines then rolled through the massive wooden doors that face the street.

Great Falls of the Passaic River, Paterson

Rogers and five other Paterson locomotive manufacturers together built nearly one-fourth of all the nineteenth-century steam engines in America.

Many Paterson steam locomotives were shipped overseas, including 144 of the 246 American locomotives used to build the Panama Canal. One of those was Old 299, which returned to Paterson in 1979 and can be seen at the rear of the Rogers Locomotive Erecting Shop. The Rogers building itself has been restored and currently houses an exhibit on the history of industry in Paterson.

From the Rogers building, continue down Spruce Street past the Union Works/Rosen Mill. Constructed in 1890 as a locomotive manufacturing plant, the building was converted to ribbon manufacturing in 1916. Just past the Union Works, the middle section of the S.U.M. raceway system leads to the right; follow the path along the raceway to where it meets McBride Avenue. Work on the original raceway system began in 1792, when the newly formed Society for the Establishment of Useful Manufactures hired Pierre L'Enfant, the French architect-engineer who designed Washington, D.C., to design a system that would channel water for power to mills constructed and operated by the S.U.M. L'Enfant left Paterson in 1793 because of differences of opinion with the S.U.M., but the raceway was finally completed in 1838, first under Peter Colt's direction, and then under that of his son Roswell.

As the raceway emerges at McBride Avenue, look across the street and to the left. The reddish rock that is exposed here is Brunswick formation sandstone, formed in Triassic times before the volcanic episodes that created the Watchung Mountains occurred. Like the sandstone of the Stockton formation found to the south, the sandstone here was quarried for use as building stone, especially during the nineteenth century. At that time, much of the quarried stone found its way into Paterson's buildings, and also into the raceway canals, which are lined with locally quarried brownstone.

Directly above the layers of sandstone can be seen the Watchung basalt, which is brownish in color in some places because of the weathering of iron-bearing minerals in the rock. Like the brownstone, basalt was also quarried to serve Paterson's industries. The pinnacle of basalt to the left of this outcrop (near the Haines Overlook Park) marks the former height of a basalt ridge, which was quarried away before the early 1900s.

Turn right onto McBride Avenue and follow it downhill to Mill Street and turn left. After passing the Franklin Mill and Essex Mill (on the left), the road bends right. The raceway emerges again here, and beyond it lies what remains of one of Paterson's most famous industries—the Colt Gun Mill. Identified today by a sign that reads Standard Dyeing and Finishing Co., this two-story building originally towered four stories and was topped by a six-story cupola bell tower. Here Samuel Colt built his first production firearms, and between 1836 and 1841, approximately 5,000 muskets, rifles, and revolvers were made here.

Swing right to follow the raceway along Van Houten Street, passing the Todd Mill and the Nightingale Mill before coming to the Phoenix Mill complex. The Phoenix Mill was operating as early as 1815, producing candlewick and cotton, later switching to linen and flax production. In 1860, Benjamin Tilt began silk production on the top floor of the factory, and by 1865 he controlled the entire structure, converting it from cotton production to silk. In the 1880s, the Phoenix Company employed 8,000 people and had 500 looms. Altogether in Paterson there were 120 silk mills with nearly 15,000 workers, producing half of the silk in the United States.

It was about this same time that the workers in the silk mills began to organize for better pay and working conditions. In 1913, organized by the Industrial Workers of the World, over 20,000 silk workers staged an industry-wide strike. During the strike the I.W.W. leaders used to meet in a bar across the street from the Phoenix Mill; this building survives as the Question Mark Bar.

The strike in some ways marked the ebbing of Paterson's industrial growth, growth that had lasted over a century and a half and had produced a variety of industrial achievements. As you return to the parking lot (backtrack along Van Houten Street and then McBride Avenue), consider that these achievements, though notable, did not come without some severe damage to the environment. The devastated traprock cliffs, the fouled waters of the Passaic, and the smoke-filled air are as much reminders of what is destructive about our use of the environment as the graceful brick and brownstone buildings are of our constructive endeavors.

# 11. Morristown National Historical Park

*Jockey Hollow Area*
Distance: 3 miles (Moderate)
Walking time: 1½ hours
Directions: Take Interstate 287 to exit 26B. Then turn right and go north on US 202, 2 miles to Templewick Rd. and turn left. The entrance to the park is 1½ miles ahead on the right. Park in the main parking lot in front of the visitor's center. The park is open 9:00 A.M. to 5:00 P.M. every day except Thanksgiving Day and New Year's Day.

When George Washington led the Continental Army into winter quarters in Morristown in 1777, he could not have chosen a better place to rest and reassemble his army, which was weary from hard-won battles at Trenton and Princeton. From the prosperous farms nearby, wheat, corn, oats, vegetables, and fruits were available. Much of the land was forested and could supply firewood and timber for huts. Nearby creeks provided ample fresh water. Mines and furnaces to the north supplied iron to be worked into tools and weapons. A mill on the Whippany River was a ready source of gunpowder made from saltpeter, sulfur, and charcoal.

The most important resources that were provided by the land around Morristown were the Watchung Mountains east of town. This double ridge of massive basalt formed natural ramparts whose passes could be easily defended. Lookouts posted on ridge tops could readily detect any movement by the British, who were camped in New York City, thirty miles away. Confident that the enemy could not attack, Washington used Morristown as a rallying place, in the winter of both 1777 and 1779.

The encampments of the Continental Army were lo-

N

To Interstate 287

cated about four miles south of Morristown in Jockey
Hollow. Nearly 1,000 acres of land here is preserved as
part of the Morristown National Historical Park. The area
today looks much as it did when the Continental Army
arrived there in the winter of 1777. This walk tells the
story of that army as it struggled to survive.

Begin at the visitor's center, where one can obtain trail
maps and other information. The trail maps are not dis-

played, but can be requested from the interpreter at the center. Before leaving the visitor's center be sure to look at the mural depicting the encampment.

Follow the wood-chip-lined path to the Wick Farm. Though the Wick Farm has been restored because of its role in American military history (the house served as Gen. Arthur St. Clair's headquarters during the 1779–1780 encampment), its richness lies in the glimpse it provides us of a prosperous family of that day. By 1780, the farm included 1,400 acres, most of it woodland, which provided lumber and firewood. The cleared acreage yielded a wide variety of products to meet the family's needs: cereals, fruits, vegetables, and livestock.

Look out over the well-kept orchard and imagine children harvesting apples in October. The herb garden next to the house has well-labeled plants that give an idea of how Mrs. Wick would have livened up a ham or turkey. Passing the barn in back, one is reminded of the winter of 1779, when not a few of Henry Wick's sheep, geese, and pigs were pilfered by the starving soldiers of the Continental Army.

Continue straight past the barn on the dirt road and look for a trail marker and map posted on the right. The trail leading into the woods takes you through a young deciduous wood predominantly of white ash and black locust, with some stands of beech. It is interesting to note that in describing the cutting of these same woods in 1779, officers and soldiers referred to the woods as being of "oak, chestnut, and walnut." Today, no mature chestnuts can be found because of the blight that eliminated them earlier in this century. However, what has become of the oak and walnut?

The walnuts the soldiers wrote about were really hickory trees of three species: pignut, mockernut, and shagbark. Almost all of the early settlers used the term walnut to describe the hickories. The oaks referred to

Restored Revolutionary War soldiers' cabins, Morristown National Historical Park

were indeed oaks, most likely white, red, and scarlet oaks, but both the oaks and hickories are poorly represented in the contemporary forest cover.

The forest here is actually in an early stage of succession which will eventually lead back to the type of forest described by the Continental soldiers. After these woods had been cut to supply the soldiers' needs, they began to return, only to be cut repeatedly in the 1800s to produce charcoal. Now that this land is protected from this type of human disturbance, the white ash and black locust that are presently so common will eventually yield to oaks and hickories.

An interesting change in the wildlife associated with these forests accompanies this forest transition. Woodpeckers are not as numerous in these woods today as they will be when a mature forest containing more dead trees provides better feeding and nesting sites. Mammals will profit from mature trees also. The hollow centers the trees develop as they age will provide shelter for gray squirrels, flying squirrels, raccoons, and opossums.

One-half mile from the start, the trail crosses a fire road and forks. Go to the left here. Notice how many of the young ash and locust trees are covered with grape and poison ivy vines struggling to get their share of the sunlight. Another ½ mile further, the trail emerges into a grassy area. In front of you is the hillside where over 1,000 log huts once stood. The soldiers constructed these huts themselves, as well as the bunks, tables, and chairs that furnished them. Each hut was fourteen-by-sixteen feet square and six and one-half feet high, and housed twelve men. Log chimneys covered with plaster rose up from fireplaces built of stone. Fueled by locally cut timber, the fires in these hearths cooked the soldiers' food and provided them with a minimal amount of warmth.

After inspecting the huts, follow the trail to the right to an interpretive sign which describes the encampments that have long since disappeared, having been reclaimed by the woods. All that remains are the stone hearths, which can be found scattered throughout the area. One of these hearths lies a few feet to the right of the interpretive sign. Bear left as you leave the sign, and then bear right at the T at the top of the hill. The red and yellow blazes you see on the trees here are part of a gypsy-moth-control experiment being conducted by the New Jersey Department of Agriculture.

At the next T, bear right again and watch your footing as you descend the hill. Huge tulip trees dot the slope here. In May and June, the large tuliplike orange flowers are conspicuous. These flowers give way to artichokelike fruits, which in winter provide food for gray squirrels, purple finches, and evening grosbeaks. Below the tulip

Apple orchard, Morristown National Historical Park

trees, spicebush becomes common; its yellow flowers bloom early in spring.

Shortly the trail emerges onto an open field known as the Grand Parade. Cross over to the right where there are a number of interpretive displays. This quiet meadow once rang with the sounds of military drills. Inspections took place here almost daily. Here, guards received their assignments, offenders were punished, and the troops heard general orders. Occasionally military displays were conducted here for Washington's guests, as when Lafayette came to Morristown.

Cross the road and turn onto the fire trail and follow this ¼ mile to a parking area. Follow along the back of the lot to the sign saying Aqueduct Trail and reenter the woods. After crossing the fire road, the trail bears to the left, where it becomes flanked by Christmas fern and a small stream. This stream is one of those that supplied the Continental Army with water during the encampment.

Almost a century later, this and other streams in Jockey Hollow were impounded to supply water to the growing village of Morristown. The trail comes upon an old brick cistern which was part of these waterworks.

For an interesting detour, continue along the stream for about ¼ mile. The rubble along the left of the trail is actually the remains of one of the waterworks impoundments. When the trail comes to a low hill of jumbled rock, stop and take a closer look. These rocks are tailings from a mica mine which was worked during the 1800s. Before glass came into use, mica sheets, called isinglass, were used as windows.

Retrace your steps to the cistern, and follow the trail back to the fire road. This road leads you back to the trail to the Wick Farm, the start of your walk.

# 12. Lord Stirling Park

*The Edge of the Great Swamp*
Distance: 3½ miles (Easy)
Walking time: 1¾ hours
Directions: Take Interstate 287 to exit 27. Follow N. Maple Ave. to Basking Ridge and continue on S. Maple Ave. Turn left onto Lord Stirling Rd. and go 1 mile. Look for the Interpretive and Education Building on left. The center and trails are open 9:00 A.M. to 4:00 P.M. on weekdays, and the trails are open 10:00 A.M. to 4:00 P.M. on Saturday, 1:00 P.M. to 5:00 P.M. on Sunday.

An extensive boardwalk system, observation towers and blinds, and an attractive new visitor's center make this walk unique. The area, Lord Stirling Park, is administered by the Somerset County Park Commission, which has built almost 8,000 feet of six-foot-wide boardwalk and many wooden bridges to make it easy to penetrate the inaccessible Great Swamp basin. The park gets its name from colonial times when the land was a small part of the vast holdings of William Alexander, the lord of Stirling, who served as a general in the Continental Army.

Lord Stirling Park lies on the western edge of the Great Swamp basin. The basin is the remnant of Glacial Lake Passaic, which formed approximately 12,000 years ago when water from the melting glacier became trapped between the retreating Wisconsin ice sheet to the north, and the Watchung Mountains to the south and east. Layer upon layer of clay sediments were laid down at the bottom of this glacial lake, making the soil impervious to water and thus preventing drainage. As the ice sheet retreated further, a gap near what is today Paterson was uncorked, allowing the waters to flow out, creating a series of low-lying minilakes. However, because of the to-

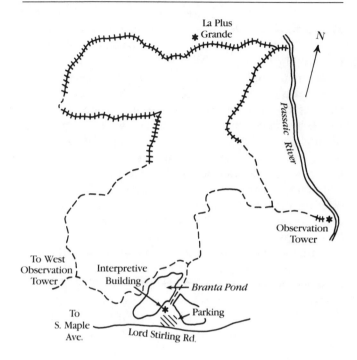

pography and the impervious clay soil, these minilakes
never drained completely, but like lakes everywhere
slowly filled in with silt and organic matter.

Before starting your walk, stop at the Interpretive
Building which houses a library, an exhibit hall, and a
book and gift shop. (One can even rent binoculars here.)
Before you leave the building, take note of the sign that
lists the day's trail conditions. Despite the extensive
boardwalk, portions of the trail can be quite soggy at
times.

Follow the yellow and red trail over Branta Pond, a
man-made pond which serves as home to many muskrat
and Canada geese. Note the "island" at the center of the
pond where a small weather station is located. In the
fields to the right of the trail here can be seen a variety of

birds that prefer this type of habitat: eastern kingbirds, brown thrashers, meadowlarks, field sparrows, and occasionally, bluebirds.

Stay on the red trail; soon you cross a wooden bridge. This area is dominated by red maple, which is a common woody pioneer in the swamp forest. Before long, the woods become denser, the maples and scattered gray birch giving way to white oak, black birch, and some beech trees. This is one of the areas in which the water table is slightly further below the surface and the soil is consequently drier. Another tree characteristic of these drier pockets appears here also: the shagbark hickory, easily recognized by its light-colored bark flaking in long, loose strips.

At the boardwalk, turn right to follow the unmarked trail to the observation tower. Continue to a T and turn right, where you emerge into an open field full of goldenrod and occasional hawthorns. The hawthorns make this field excellent winter habitat for northern shrikes, also known as butcher birds. These birds have no talons, and so they impale their prey on a barbed-wire fence or sharp thorn such as that of the hawthorn, to make it easier to tear it apart. Small birds and rodents are their usual prey, and if you look sharply, you may find one impaled on these thorns during the fall or winter. This field and the others in the park are visible reminders that the area was farmed at one time—up until the late 1950s, in fact.

Bear left along the mowed path on the edge of the field and follow it to a boardwalk that reenters the woods. The observation tower here looks east across the Passaic River, which is the principal drainage for the Great Swamp basin. The river is flanked by willows, ash, and red maple, with reed grass and cattails on the floodplain beyond. In summer, the pink and white blossoms of swamp rose mallow make this a lovely spot. Spend a few minutes looking for

American bitterns and other herons before retracing your steps.

At the T bear right instead of returning to the boardwalk crossed earlier. As you pass a large standing chestnut hulk on the right, notice the foliage at the top. This may at first appear to be a final attempt at growth by this venerable tree, but the foliage really belongs to a less venerable plant—poison ivy. The thick vine can be seen leading from the base of the tree.

The trail then skirts the edge of a marsh that is drying out and becomes a boardwalk again. The boardwalk crosses a series of rivulets lined with arrowhead and pickerelweed and then passes some thickets of red osier and silky dogwood and arrowwood. Two species of skullcaps—marsh and mad dog—which are violet-flowered members of the mint family, are common along here. The curious parasitic plant—dodder—also grows here. Lacking any green leaves, its orange stems look like a mass of tangled fishing line.

The trail leads back to the river for one more look. Be especially sure to take this look in August when the scarlet of cardinal flowers brightens the river bank. Turn around and follow the boardwalk away from the river, bearing right this time, and emerge into La Plus Grande, a magnificent area of open water ringed by a lovely freshwater marsh. Broad- and narrow-leaved cattails yield to plants such as meadowsweet, willow, and swamp rose. Buttonbush, a semiaquatic shrub whose small white flowers are clustered in ball-like heads, is abundant here also. Its blossoms are visited by scores of nectar-seeking bees and butterflies in mid-summer.

At your feet are a number of interesting plants also. Arrowhead and its smaller-flowered relative water plantain, ground nut, and wild mint all grow along the boardwalk here. In the thickets nearby can be seen catbirds, cedar waxwings, and long-billed marsh wrens. Green her-

Boardwalk, Lord Stirling Park

ons and great blue herons stalk fish and frogs in the waters, and at dusk in August one can pause to watch dozens of nighthawks winging their way overhead.

The boardwalk enters different woods from what has been seen so far. Pin oak is the main tree here, with a lower layer of ironwood, and below this are blueberry bushes. Ironwood, also known as hornbeam or musclewood, has distinctive smooth gray bark which is stretched over a muscular-looking trunk. This small tree is a common member of the understory in areas with moist, rich soil. The ground underneath the ironwood is covered with hummocks of sedge. Continue through these woods to a fork in the boardwalk and go right. Great crested flycatchers can often be heard overhead along this part of the trail. Along the ground, ovenbirds and occasional thrushes are heard.

Just after this section of boardwalk ends, go right onto a grassy lane. This leads past an American beech tree on the left, which has recently been struck by lightning. The air around a bolt of lightning is heated to such a high temperature that a struck tree is actually blown apart by the force of the expanding water vapor inside the tree. Occasionally, bits of charred lichen, fungus, and bark can be found near the struck tree.

Just beyond this tree, go right onto the red trail, which leads onto a boardwalk again and then comes to a huge white oak along the left of the trail. This oak is probably over 300 years old. A forester would call it a wolf tree—typically a large short-trunked, spreading tree that 'wolfs" more than its share of the light from the canopy overhead. Such trees grow in open areas, and this one gives evidence that the area around it may have been open pastureland for many years.

Continue on the red trail to where an unmarked trail joins it from the left. To the left of the trail near here is an area where many small depressions in the soil can be seen. These were created when the previous owners of the land sold live trees to be used in landscaping the 1965 World's Fair grounds in New York. The trees were selected because the high water table in this area causes the roots to grow close to the surface, making the trees easier to remove.

Continue on the red trail past Bridge 5 and bear right onto the unmarked trail. This trail leads through an abandoned field ringed by goldenrod and staghorn sumac, and passes a small semipermanent pond on the right. In dry periods, one can see the reddish rock that lines the bottom of this pond. A pile of this rock can also be seen to the left of the pond. The pond was excavated during efforts to drain the area many years ago. What makes the pond worth a stop is that it exposes the rock that underlies all of the Great Swamp basin: soft shale and sandstone, which are brownish red in color. The sediments that make up this rock were deposited about 190 million years ago during the period when dinosaurs roamed this area. This rock was of importance to New York City and other eastern cities in the late 1800s, as it was quarried for building stones. The brownstone of Manhattan's and Brooklyn's brownstone houses is actually red sandstone quarried in this area.

Continue through the field toward the observation tower visible ahead. Late summer flowers along here include wild bergamot and dense blazing star. Stop at the observation tower and look out over the fields you have just walked through. Woodchucks and cottontail rabbits can frequently be seen here. Kingbirds sally out from perches in the field to snap up flying insects, and the "wicker" call of the flicker is heard as it scratches about looking for ants.

Pass through the orchard ahead and then take a sharp left through the thicket. Follow this trail through a small section of woods and along the margin of an abandoned field until you return to the red trail. Bear right here and follow the trail to the blind on the edge of Branta Pond. Canada geese and wood ducks are most frequently seen on the pond; from this blind they can be easily observed at close range. From here, follow the red trail back to the Interpretive Building.

# 13. Herrontown Woods

Distance: 1¼ miles (Easy)
Walking time: 2 hours
Directions: From the north, take NJ 27 to Princeton, from the south US 206. (Both of these roads become Nassau St. in the center of Princeton.) Turn right (left if coming from the south) onto Snowden Lane and follow the signs to Herrontown Woods. The area is open 8:00 A.M. to 5:00 P.M. from November to April, 8:00 A.M. to 9:00 P.M. from May to October.

---

The forest of Herrontown Woods, like all forests, is a product of a variety of environmental factors such as soil type, topography, and geology. In addition, as with so much of New Jersey's landscape, the patterns of the contemporary forest have their origins in changes wrought by man's use of the land. Herrontown Woods, though unspectacular, is an excellent place to gain a better understanding of how these factors interact, as the mosaic of forest types found here occurs in a small area.

Begin your walk at the red-blazed trail near the entrance to the parking lot. (There is a trail map posted next to the trail entrance.) This trail immediately enters a plantation of red pines and then shortly emerges to turn right across an old stone wall. The young woods along this part of the trail are mainly made up of white ash and red maple, two of the most important pioneers to invade abandoned land in the New Jersey Piedmont. Both the pine plantation and the young forest here are growing on farmland abandoned around the turn of the century; the stone walls attest to the fact that this land was formerly a hayfield or pasture.

The trail emerges into a clearing which is another remnant of the once active farm. Take the blue-blazed trail

91

which leaves from the right of the clearing next to another wooden trail map. The soil along this portion of the trail is noticeably more moist than in the previous section, and the moist conditions allow many of the trees to reach fairly large size. The dominant trees are oaks—mainly white, black, and red—although they are joined occasionally by hickories and tulip trees. Below this mature forest canopy grow flowering dogwood and ironwood, and below these there is a shrub layer of spicebush, which thrives in the deep, moist soil.

A variety of wildflowers can be seen on the floor of this mature forest in early spring. Many of these plants do most of their growing and flowering before the canopy leafs out and makes the forest floor too dark for active growth. One of the earliest of these spring wildflowers is the spring beauty. It bears two grasslike leaves and a cluster of flower buds arranged in a "fiddlehead." The pink or white five-petaled flowers bloom sequentially, each flower lasting just one day. Another common wildflower is Solomon's seal, which is recognized by its large, curved, single stem with smooth, oval leaves arranged alternately along it. Solomon's seal's yellowish, bell-shaped flowers appear in May, growing in pairs from the axils of the leaves. Mayapple, skunk cabbage, jack-in-the-pulpit, and other wildflowers preferring moist sites are also seen here in the spring.

As the trail begins to climb, the soil and the overlying vegetation can be seen to change dramatically. The wet spots that allowed plants like mayapple and skunk cabbage to thrive on the lower slope are no longer present, and the more drought-tolerant maple-leaf viburnum replaces the moisture-loving spicebush as the dominant shrub. Overhead, ironwood has dropped from the understory, and sweet gum and tulip tree have disappeared from the canopy. The large boulders scattered through the woods suggest the stoniness of the underlying soil.

These dark gray, angular boulders are a clue to the nature of the ridge that the trail has been ascending. The boulders are pieces of diabase, the rock that lies beneath all but the southeast corner of Herrontown Woods. Like the other volcanic rocks that are found in the Piedmont of New Jersey, this diabase was formed in late Triassic times, when volcanic activity forced great flows of molten rock up through the surrounding layers of sandstone and shale. This molten rock cooled slowly beneath the earth's surface, and did not become exposed until much later, after millions of years of erosion had stripped away the soft sedimentary rock, leaving the diabase as a ridge. The diabase ridge here at Herrontown Woods is known as Rocky Hill, but it is geologically part of the same sill (an intrusive rock that follows parallel to the beds of the intruded layers of rock), that forms the Palisades along the Hudson River.

The trail comes out to a swath cut through the woods for a gas pipeline right-of-way, then reenters the woods again. About 100 yards ahead to the left of the trail can be seen an old traprock quarry, marked by an angular block of diabase with a small excavation in front of it. Closer inspection of the diabase outcrop will reveal evidence of the quarrying: the straight, narrow grooves on the face of the outcrop are marks caused by a star drill, which was used by quarrymen to fracture the rock. In the late nineteenth century, diabase was removed from quarries all along this ridge to be used as crushed rock for road building and other purposes. Today, the Kingston Trap Rock Company still quarries diabase nearby for road metal and concrete aggregate. Dump trucks are seen constantly on the roads around Kingston, roaring to and from the quarry, picking up loads of traprock for construction projects.

The trail continues along the top of the diabase ridge, through an area where the trees are somewhat smaller and more closely spaced than on the slope below, indicating that it may have been cut more recently. Red, white, and black oaks again are the principal trees, but in some places pin oak is also seen. The leaf of the black oak has an oval outline, cut by two to three deep sinuses on each side. Each of the five to seven lobes of the black-oak leaf has several points. The black bark is ridged, with widely spaced furrows between the ridges. The red oak is similar to the black oak, but its leaves are not quite as stout, and its bark is gray with wide reddish furrows. Do not be disturbed if you find certain trees that are intermediate between the two species: these trees hybridize freely with one another, and their progeny hybridize occasionally also. This mixed oak forest soon yields to a "new" forest, however. Sweet gum becomes the dominant tree; this is

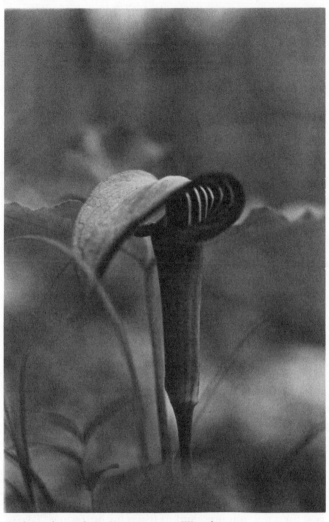

Jack-in-the-pulpit, Herrontown Woods

especially easy to observe in the fall, when the trail is littered with the fallen fruits. Growing with the sweet gum are black oaks, red maple, shagbark and pignut hickory, and below these grows a shrub layer of blackhaw, a relative of maple-leaf viburnum. Its egg-shaped, five-toothed leaves look much like those of the black cherry tree, but are distinguished by being oppositely arranged. Its blackish fruits, which are eaten by foxes, ruffed grouse, and occasionally by people, appear in early fall.

A small grove of beech trees is traversed before the trail reaches a very moist area near the headwaters of a small stream that drains this ridgetop. The red maple trees (often called swamp maples, suggesting their affinity for wet areas) that abound here are distinctive in that many have roots that protrude a few inches above the ground. Such adventitious roots occur often in areas where trees are seasonally inundated by water. The moistness of this area is also indicated by the reappearance of ironwood in the understory and spicebush as the main shrub.

The trail reaches a junction with the red-blazed trail; bear right onto this trail and then swing left almost immediately onto a trail blazed with red and black markers. This trail runs parallel to the stream for about ⅛ mile before emerging onto the pipeline right-of-way again. To rejoin the trail, bear left toward the yellow posts and then turn right to enter the woods.

The trail leads downhill a short distance and then joins a yellow-blazed trail; bear left here. This trail crosses the stream and leads through a large boulder field. At one point the trail skirts the edge of a huge traprock boulder that has fractured to form a concave seat in the face of the rock. In spring and summer, this is a good place to sit and rest for a few minutes, and to listen for bird songs. Two of the most common songs you're likely to hear are those of the wood thrush and the ovenbird. The wood thrush's song is one of the most beautiful of North American bird-songs; its rich, flutelike melody prompted Henry David

Thoreau to write: "Whenever a man hears it he is young, and Nature is in her spring; wherever he hears it, it is a new world and a free country, and the gates of heaven are not shut against him."

The ovenbird's song is less melodious than the wood thrush's, but it is equally distinctive. An emphatic "teacher, teacher, teacher" is repeated rapidly by the ovenbird in an insistent crescendo. The ovenbird, like the wood thrush, is more often heard than seen. Both are colored much like the leaf litter that carpets the forest floor, where they spend most of their time foraging quietly for insects. Despite these similarities, the two birds are quite different taxonomically, the wood thrush belonging to the thrush family, while the ovenbird (which gets its name from the domed, oven-shaped nest it builds on the ground), belongs to the wood warbler family.

The trail comes to a junction a short distance ahead; bear right and follow it through another boulder-strewn area. Many of the oaks here—mainly red and black—are quite large, having perhaps been protected from the most recent logging by the steep slope and rocky terrain. This and other diabase and basalt ridges throughout New Jersey's Piedmont were important sources for firewood from the late eighteenth through the mid-nineteenth century, since almost all of the flatlands had been cleared for farming. The ridge that is now Herrontown Woods not only supplied fuel for farmers' stoves, but is said to have also been cut to provide firewood for some of the Princeton University faculty. Remember that in those days, everyone, farmer and academic alike, heated with wood.

The yellow trail eventually meets a green-blazed trail; turn right and follow this trail out to the stream. The trail has begun to level out somewhat, and this fact, combined with the reappearance of the stone walls, suggests that you have left the diabase ridge behind and emerged onto the low-lying, flatland of the Brunswick shale and sandstone. Careful observation along the streambed will confirm this, as pieces of reddish sedimentary rock can be seen. Many of the gray rocks that lie in the stream, though they appear like the volcanic rock diabase, are actually sedimentary in origin also. Being at the edge of the molten magma when it was intruded, some of the soft red shale in this area was baked to become the hard, gray rock seen here, called hornfels.

Continue following this trail until it meets a red-blazed trail, then bear right. The parking lot lies a short distance ahead, through the pine plantation.

# 14. Charles Rogers Sanctuary and Princeton Institute Woods

Distance: 2 miles (Easy)
Walking time: 1 hour
Directions: Take US 1 to Princeton and exit at Alexander
St. Continue until you cross the Delaware and Raritan
Canal and take the first left, West Drive. Bear left at the
fork, then park on the right near the observation tower.

---

Because the Piedmont in New Jersey is so uniform topo-
graphically, its interest lies in other features of the landscape—its forests, animals, and bird life. On this walk,
many of these features are readily observed, as it begins at
a freshwater marsh, leads through a lovely riparian woodland, and concludes in a section of upland forest. In
spring, this diversity of habitat is attractive to northward
migrating birds, especially warblers, making these two
adjacent sanctuaries an excellent place to observe the
spring migration.

Before beginning your walk, make your way to the top
of the small observation tower that overlooks the marsh.
The principal plant here is the familiar cattail, followed by
pickerelweed, a stout plant with fleshy, arrowhead-shaped
leaves, which emerges from the shallower waters of the
marsh. Pickerelweed is easily recognized in summer by its
dense spike of violet blue flowers.

By late summer, the open waters of the marsh are covered by duckweeds, a group of small green aquatic plants.
Common duckweed is by far the most abundant, but it is
joined here by at least two other species, including the
tiny, almost granular appearing *Wolffia*—the smallest of
all North American flowering plants. As their name suggests, duckweeds are a favorite food of some surface-
feeding ducks, including mallards, blue-winged teal, and

wood ducks, all of which are commonly seen on the
marsh.

Along with the ducks, a variety of other animals can be
seen on or above the marsh. Turtles sun themselves on
tussock sedge hummocks, herons stalk frogs in the shal-
lows, and redwing blackbirds sing "o-ka-reee" from the
cattails. Overhead in fall, waves of blue jays, blackbirds,
and other birds can be seen as they wing their way south.

From the observation tower, walk out to the road, turn
right, and follow it to the Water Company parking lot. The
trail enters the woods from the right-hand corner of the
lot. It follows along Stony Brook, while it is flanked on the
right by the marsh. The forest here is made up of trees
that thrive in the moist bottomland soil along the brook.
Silver maples and box elder are two such trees. Box elder,
also known as ash-leaf maple, is a small to medium-sized
tree identified by its compound leaves, which usually bear
three leaflets. In fall and winter, its fruit—the paired
"keys" typical of the genus—identify it unmistakably as
a maple.

Away from the brook, the most common tree is the pin

oak, a handsome tree which is familiar to many because of its frequent use in ornamental plantings. Pin oak is identified by its deeply cut, pointed leaves which resemble those of the scarlet oak, though they are somewhat smaller. The tree gets its name from the fact that some of its branches are usually stubby and pinlike. Also characteristic of the pin oak are its tangled lower branches, which typically point toward the ground.

The trail swings right along the brook, where it passes sweet-smelling spicebush and sinewy ironwood trees. A variety of herbaceous plants thrives in the wet soil below: spring beauty, mayapple, jack-in-the-pulpit, skunk cabbage, and others. In the fall, woodland asters of various species are conspicuous along the trail.

The damp alluvial soil of this bottomland forest is rich with earthworms, making it a likely place to see the American woodcock, which feeds almost exclusively on earthworms. The woodcock uses its long, prehensile bill to probe for, and then capture, the worms. This compact bird is magnificently camouflaged, and often permits close approach before exploding from the forest floor with whistling wings. In late March or early April, woodcocks are particularly conspicuous, not feeding here in the bottomland forest, but performing their elaborate courtship ritual on the edge of nearby fields. The male's loud nasal "peents" are followed by a spiraling takeoff and ascent, after which the bird swoops down to its takeoff point amid a series of strange warblings.

The trail bends to the left, passes a small suspension footbridge, and continues to follow the brook. Box elders lean out from the bank and occasional sycamores tower overhead. Hickories and ashes are also prominent in this riparian woodland. The ash found here is the green ash, identified by its tightly furrowed bark, its opposite twig arrangement, and its compound leaves bearing five to nine leaflets. It is very difficult to distinguish from the white ash, which is more common in upland areas. In spring, the flowers of white ash appear before the leaves, while those of green ash appear after the leaf buds have opened; this is one way to tell the two apart where they do occur together.

Just before the trail bears right to follow the edge of a cornfield, it passes another common bottomland tree— the river birch. After the trail turns, however, the river birch, sycamores, box elders, and silver maples are left behind as the forest begins to include more upland species. Sweet gum, sassafras, and tulip trees are all common. Many of the trees are covered with vines, particularly wild grape, honeysuckle, and poison ivy. Another vine, found mainly along the small rivulets that drain toward Stony Brook, is the Canada moonseed. It is identified by its large, shallowly lobed leaves and its clusters of small white flowers, which develop into black fruits resembling wild grapes. These fruits should not be eaten, however, as they are mildly poisonous.

The trail soon reaches the pipeline right-of-way; turn right to follow this path. Just after you turn, you pass a catalpa tree on the left side of the trail. This tree's large heart-shaped leaves, showy white flowers, and long, slender fruit pods make it readily identifiable. A native of the Gulf Coast, the fast-growing catalpa was planted widely in the northeast for fence posts. Like many other alien plants, it has since escaped from cultivation, which accounts for its presence here.

In spring, the woods here are alive with warblers. These small, insectivorous birds tend to follow watercourses having a north-south orientation as they head north to their breeding grounds. Their northward migration through the riparian woodlands is "timed" to coincide with the hatching of the millions of caterpillars that feed voraciously on the green forest canopy. Redstarts, yellow-throated, cerulean, Cape May, Canada, chestnut-sided, black-throated blue, black-throated green, bay-breasted, blackburnian, blackpoll, black and white, and

Cattails, Charles Rogers Sanctuary

myrtle warblers—their names indicate the variety of these jewellike birds that can be seen here in the spring.

One of the migrating warblers that stays and makes its nest on the ground amid the sweet gums, tulip trees, and maples is the Kentucky warbler, which is near the edge of its range here. Because it forages close to the ground, the Kentucky is difficult to see except when it betrays its presence by singing its loud "churree-churree-churree" song from a low perch.

Just past the intersection of the path with a foot trail, the woods change dramatically; the white pine and quaking aspen here suggest a relatively recent disturbance of the forest. Quaking aspen grows on all types of disturbed sites: clear-cut areas, burned land, and even along highways in the sterile mineral soil. It is recognized by its smooth chalk white to yellowish green bark, and by its small grayish green rounded leaves that "quake" in even the slightest breeze.

The trail passes a wide path (actually a firebreak) and then follows through a plantation of pine trees. The dry, needle-strewn floor of this pine plantation is a sharp contrast to the damp, thickly vegetated floor of the riparian woods traversed earlier. A short distance past the firebreak, a trail leads left into a small field. Walk straight through this field, past the red barn, to the parking lot. On the left is a sign identifying the woods you have just passed through as belonging to the Institute for Advanced Study, a research institute composed of scholars from all over the world.

To return to your car, turn right onto Hardin Road, follow it to Springdale Road, and turn right, which leads you back to the parking area near the marsh. In the spring, the birding is excellent along this stretch of road.

# The Delaware River Valley

Delaware River, near Stockton

## 15. Delaware and Raritan Canal State Park

*Bull's Island*
Distance: 2¼ miles (Easy)
Walking time: 1 hour
Directions: From the north take Interstate 287 south to
Interstate 78. Go west to County Rd. 523 and take it
south about 23 miles to Stockton. Proceed north on NJ 29
and look for Delaware and Raritan Canal St. Pk. sign on
left. From the south, take US 206 to Trenton and then NJ
29 to Bull's Island. Turn left at park entrance and park in
the lot just beyond the ranger station.

Bull's Island is not really an island in the true geographical sense. It is, rather, a man-made island, created in the
1830s when the Delaware and Raritan Canal was built.
Although not a true island, Bull's Island is distinctly different from the "mainland" nearby, since the Delaware
and Raritan Canal sliced through the area where the
floodplain forest of the Delaware River gives way to upland forest. This walk takes you under the canopy of a
magnificent floodplain forest as well as out above a lovely
stretch of the Delaware River.

From the parking lot, walk back toward the canal and
turn right onto the footpath; this path is somewhat overgrown in a few places. Long pants are recommended,
since one of the plants that often encroaches upon the
trail is the stinging nettle, whose coarse stinging hairs can
cause painful irritation. The plant is most easily recognized by these hairs, which cover both the hollow stem
and the coarsely toothed, heart-shaped leaves. In summer,
the stinging nettle has tiny greenish flowers clustered
along stalks that rise from the leaf axils.

Path

Canal

Ranger's
House

Delaware River

Parking

Footbridge

N

While the stinging nettle causes skin irritation, another
plant that is found along this trail is often used to cure it.
This is the jewelweed or spotted touch-me-not, which in
summer bears pendant yellow flowers that have a curled
spur at the rear. These flowers are spotted with varying
amounts of red. If you crush the plant's succulent stem, a
juice is exuded; this juice can be spread on the skin to
relieve itching from poison ivy and insect bites.

If you take this walk in October, you may notice the
jewelweed for another reason. Its seeds mature in spring-
loaded pods which snap open when touched to eject and
distribute the seeds—thus its other common name. It is
almost impossible to walk this trail without brushing
against these seed pods, and after the first startling encounter with them, one becomes accustomed to their
constant popping.

Continue along the canal, which in this section is
topped by trees arching toward the water. The predomi-
nant trees here are silver maple and river birch, both
commonly found in bottomland forests such as this. Silver maple is identified by its six-inch, deeply cleft leaves
which have serrated margins. The underside of the foliage
is whitish gray, and often shows when the leaves are
blown by the wind.

River birch is more easily distinguished by its bark than
by its leaves. The shaggy bark varies from smooth reddish

brown flakes on the youngest branches to rough, almost black, plates on the lower trunk. Its leaves are wedge shaped, and more pointed than those of the more familiar black, white, or yellow birches.

The river birch is important to a number of birds which breed on the island, supplying both nesting material and a site upon which to build the nest. Some of the birds of the bottomland forest prefer to nest near, or even over, the water, and the river birch often provides such a site. Its shreddy bark is a major constituent of the nests of some of these birds. This is true of the nests of the yellow-throated and cerulean warblers, and the blue-gray gnatcatcher, which also uses catkins from the river birch in building its nest.

All three of these birds are near the northern limit of their range here, and this makes Bull's Island a frequent stop for many birdwatchers. Another species near its northern limit, but which is more often seen than heard along here is the Acadian flycatcher, whose loud "peet-suh" call is sure to attract attention. The Acadian flycatcher has a great affinity for streams and brooks, and its nest usually hangs from a low branch out over the water.

You may have noticed how silty the soil is along the trail—a consequence of the nature of the floodplain and the floodplain forest. Floodplains are well-defined, flat valleys that are periodically flooded. When this flooding occurs, friction along the river's banks causes the rising waters to slow down and drop some of the sediment they are carrying. The largest sediments, sand and pebbles, are dropped closest to the banks, while the finer particles (silt) are carried to the outer reaches of the floodplain, where they are deposited. As a result, the area adjacent to the river is higher and better drained than the outer area, which tends to be waterlogged much of the time.

The footpath eventually gets wider and is paved with cobblestones; this is the remains of an old road, which ran parallel to the canal. Continue on this path to where the trail ends at a small cement aqueduct. In times when the Delaware is low, you can walk out onto the exposed shallow bank and look upriver. This bank is covered with loosestrife and willow, which can tolerate even more moisture than the plants of the floodplain behind. While surveying the river from here, you may spy a belted kingfisher scanning the water from an overhanging perch or plunging headlong to catch a fish. This handsome bird is blue gray above and white below. The male has a blue gray belt across the breast, and the female is similar but in addition has a chestnut band below. The kingfisher's large head, bushy crest, daggerlike bill, and raucous call further distinguish it.

Backtrack along the footpath, taking note of the many fallen trees along the way. With the abundant moisture available to these trees, most do not need deep taproots, and the periodic inundation the floodplain receives often knocks these shallow-rooted trees over. A variety of vines covers the fallen trees: poison ivy, Virginia creeper, bittersweet, and wild grape. Some of these trees are elms that have been killed by Dutch elm disease. Although we think of the elm as a widespread tree, this is because it is widely planted as an ornamental on lawns and along streets. In its natural setting, the American elm prefers the rich moist soil of the floodplain. A number of elms on this end of the island are still standing, though dead, and these snags provide a home for wildlife. The most beautiful resident of these gray hulks is the golden orange prothonotary warbler, which is unique among warblers in that it nests in tree cavities. Some ornithologists believe that this is an adaptation to habitats like floodplains, where cavities are numerous, but where dense bushes— the usual warbler nesting site—are scarce.

In spring, the spicebush's yellow flowers brighten the lower layer of this dark forest. Below the spicebush, two

Raven Rock, near Bull's Island

flowers of the arum family are common. Skunk cabbage, familiar to everyone, thrives in the wet soil of the flood-plain. Its flower, which can be seen as early as February and March, is enclosed in a shell-like spathe, mottled and varying in color from green to purple brown. Inside, the strange-looking flowers are borne on a heavy, rounded stem called a spadix. Flies and other pollinators are at-tracted to the flower by the plant's strong odor.

The other common arum here is jack-in-the-pulpit, which is recognized by its pinnately compound leaf sug-gestive of poison ivy. Like the skunk cabbage's flower, the jack-in-the-pulpit's consists of a vertical spathe—the pulpit—wrapped around a spadix—Jack—which bears the flowers. In late summer the spathe withers, and a conical cluster of red berries is revealed.

After reaching the entrance road, continue straight across onto the grassy lane leading to an asphalt road. As you pass the ranger's house, bear right down onto the grassy path that follows the canal. In the 1800s, when the canal was operating, canal boats occasionally plied their way along here, headed south toward Trenton. This stretch of the canal was built principally to serve as a feeder to the main part of the canal, which began at Tren-ton and ran all the way to New Brunswick.

One of the main cargoes on these canal boats was Stockton formation sandstone, familiar to many as brownstone building stone. Many of the older homes in this area were built with brownstone (one can be seen just north of the park entrance on NJ 29), which also made its way into some well known buildings in cities along the canal. Old Queens at Rutgers in New Brunswick, and Nassau Hall at Princeton are two such historic buildings.

Along with the sandstone quarried at Lambertville, Stockton, and here at Raven Rock, this area provided an-other economically important rock—diabase traprock. Like the traprock of the Palisades, it is still quarried for

Box elder, Bull's Island

use as road metal and concrete aggregate. In months
when the foliage is not too dense, one of these traprock
cliffs can be seen to the right beyond the canal and NJ 29.
The village of Raven Rock gets its name from this striking
black rock outcrop.

Today, wood ducks and Canada geese replace the canal
boats, and these and other waterfowl are commonly seen
floating along the waters of the old canal. The primarily
vegetarian ducks and geese feed on the foliage and seeds
of a variety of aquatic plants which grow in and along the
canal.

The path eventually comes out to a cleared area at the
northern tip of the island. This spot offers a nice vantage
of the Delaware River, and is a good place in spring and
fall to see migrating geese, ducks, and hawks. Occasionally, an osprey will pause in its long journey to circle the
river in search of fish in the waters below.

Follow the road that leads from this cleared area, passing a line of huge sycamores flanking the river. The sycamore has distinctive mottled bark that flakes off in jigsawlike pieces, exposing the yellowish underbark. The three- to five-lobed toothed leaves and round, long-stalked fruits are equally distinctive. Although the sycamore is occasionally topped in height by the tulip tree, it is generally recognized as the most massive tree in the eastern United States. Many of the sycamores here are over 4 feet in diameter and over 100 feet tall. The Delaware Indians prized the sycamore for their dugout canoes.

After passing the small dam that spans the river, bear left and follow the road back toward the canal. The road bears right and passes the ranger's house again, and then rejoins the entrance road. Turn right and follow the road past the parking lot to the footbridge over the Delaware. From the footbridge, there is a wonderful view of the river, and of the tall trees of Bull's Island's floodplain forest. Before returning to the car, it is worth crossing over to the Pennsylvania side of the river to the lovely town of Lumberville. If you turn right after crossing the footbridge and walk along the road a short distance, you reach the site of lock 12 of the Delaware Canal, which was operated by the state of Pennsylvania between 1831 and 1858.

# 16. Washington Crossing State Park

Distance: 2½ miles (Easy)
Walking time: 1¼ hours
Directions: Take NJ 29 to NJ 546 east. Go one mile and
look for park entrance on the left. Follow signs to the
visitor's center, and park there.

In the fall of 1776, Gen. George Washington and the soldiers of the Continental Army began a retreat from Fort
Lee to Pennsylvania. In skirmish after skirmish, the Continental Army had proved no match for the well-trained
British troops, and with Washington and his army trying
to regroup across the river, the British settled into winter
quarters at Trenton. It looked to many as if the colonies
would never break free of British rule.

Then, in a daring surprise attack, the Continental Army
crossed the icy waters of the Delaware River on December 26, 1776. The army then marched to Trenton, where
they defeated the British, and, some historians believe,
turned the tide of the Revolutionary War. This walk takes
you past the spot where Washington and his army first
landed after crossing the Delaware, and along a portion
of the route the soldiers took to Trenton.

Before beginning your walk, you may wish to visit the
visitor's center, which has displays of colonial artifacts and
an audiovisual orientation to the park. From the visitor's
center, walk straight out to meet Continental Lane, the
road over which the Continental Army began its march to
Trenton in 1776. Bear left onto this lane, which is flanked
on either side by dogwood trees. The pink and white
blossoms of the dogwood make this section of the walk
particularly lovely in spring.

Follow this lane past the forest nursery on the left to
where it ends near a large stone barn. This is the Flag

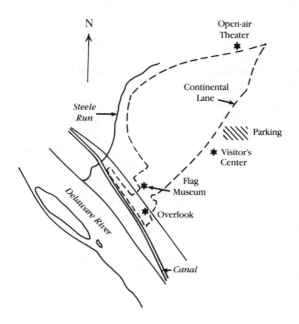

Museum, where there are displays that depict the evolution of the United States flag from the flags of the earliest explorers to that of the present day. From here, take the road that leads to the left, and then bear right onto the gravel path, which passes an overlook of the Delaware River.

The trail then leads to a pedestrian bridge; follow this bridge down to the river bank, where there is a reproduction of a wooden ferryboat like the ones used by the Continental Army in their famous river crossing.

Backtrack to the pedestrian bridge, and walk underneath it to come out by a grassy path along a narrow waterway. This is the feeder of the Delaware and Raritan Canal, which runs south from Raven Rock (see Bull's Island Walk 15) to Trenton. The feeder was built in 1834 to keep the main canal full, as well as to transport cargo. By 1870, muskrat, who constantly dug holes in the banks, and

*Washington Crossing State Park* 115

the railroads, which hauled freight faster than canal boats, had joined to put the Delaware and Raritan Canal out of business.

Follow the canal for about ⅓ mile until you reach a picnic area, then walk out to the road and turn right. A few hundred yards along on the left, enter near the white gate and walk toward the Flag Museum. As you approach the museum, look for a trail on the left, which leads into a plantation of red pines. The red pine grows naturally only in a small area in the very northern part of New Jersey, but you are likely to see it anywhere in the state, as it is planted widely for reforesting cut-over areas. The pines then grow into pure, even-aged stands like this one, which though pleasant to walk through, are biological deserts. Except for a few shade-tolerant ferns, mosses, and fungi, there is little plant life, and few animals make their home here.

The trail comes to a railing; turn right and go about 50 yards, then turn left. You pass out of the pine plantation into deciduous woods of red oak, red maple, and tulip trees. The trail comes to a creek—Steele Run—flanked by large white oaks. These oaks are extremely important to the most common mammal found in such woods, the gray squirrel, who prefers white oak acorns to any other food. Although there are many white oaks in this forest, most are fairly young and do not bear a heavy crop of acorns; in fact, the first crop does not appear until the tree is about twenty years old. It would take the acorns of fifty twenty-year-old trees to sustain a single squirrel through the winter.

As you walk along the creek, note the outcrops of layered reddish rock to your left; this is Brunswick shale, so named because of its outcropping along the Raritan River at New Brunswick. Brunswick shale began as one of the sediments laid down in the area known as the Newark basin, which was formed about 190 million years ago. At that time, large blocks of the earth's crust were lifted and

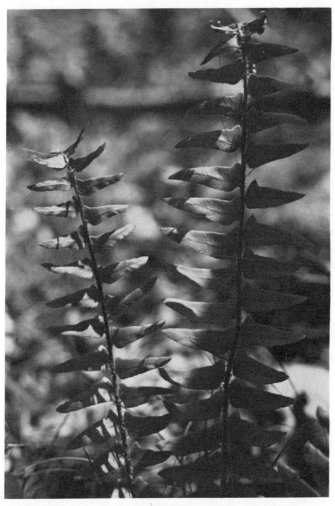

Christmas fern, Washington Crossing State Park

tilted to form mountains. Over time, thousands of feet of sediments were washed down from these mountains into the Newark basin and were deposited in broad, flat alluvial fans which later became rock. While these sediments were being laid down, dinosaurs and other long-extinct reptiles roamed the Newark basin, and coelacanths and six-foot-long amphibians swam in the Triassic swamps and ponds. Fossils of many of these ancient animals are turned up frequently, especially in the brownstone quarries scattered throughout the Newark basin.

The trail passes over a footbridge, where the stream has again exposed the underlying bedrock. An understory of dogwood and a shrub layer of witch hazel and spicebush thrive on this gentle slope, and Christmas fern is conspicuous along the ground in some places. The largest of the evergreen ferns native to this area, Christmas fern is easily recognized by the shape of its pinnae (leaflets), which look like small green Christmas stockings. This is less likely the origin of the plant's name than the fact that it is one of the few ferns that is still green at Christmas.

The trail continues past a small beech grove and a few scattered elms which still appear healthy. In the 1930s, a fungus known as Dutch elm disease was introduced to this continent, and it spread rapidly, wiping out thousands of elms throughout the country. The disease is spread from tree to tree by a native bark beetle, which picks up the fungus when it bores its hole in the bark, then carries the fungal spores with it to the next tree.

The trail passes through the Green Grove picnic area; ignore the side trails here and stay along the creek. Beyond the picnic area, the stream is flanked by hemlocks and rhododendron, and for a minute, it feels as if you are walking along a ravine along the Kittatinny Ridge. Just after passing the open-air theater to your left, the trail crosses an asphalt road, follows a brook for another 200 yards, and then emerges at Continental Lane. Turn right here and follow this trail ½ mile to reach the parking lot.

# The Inner Coastal Plain

Cattail marsh, near Cranbury
*Courtesy Robichaud and Buell*

# 17. Cheesequake State Park

Distance: 3½ miles (Moderate)
Walking time: 2 hours
Directions: Take the Garden State Parkway to exit 120. Go east on Matawan Rd. ¼ mile and turn right onto Cliffwood Ave. Turn right on Gordon Ave. and go 1 mile to the park entrance. Continue past the entrance ⅛ mile to the parking area on the left. There is a parking fee of $3.00 on weekends and $1.00 weekdays from Memorial Day to Labor Day.

Close to the sprawling metropolis of northeastern New Jersey, Cheesequake State Park preserves an extensive salt marsh, a small cedar swamp, and an interesting variety of plant and animal life. Because of its proximity to this metropolis and also to the mosquito-harboring salt marshes, it is best to visit the park in late fall or early spring, when the summertime crowds of visitors and biting insects can be avoided.

Follow the yellow-green-red-blazed trail which leads away from the parking lot through woods of white oak, sassafras, and black gum trees. To the left, a small brook follows the trail as it flows toward Cheesequake Creek. Flanked by sweet pepperbush, this shallow brook is reminiscent of the cripples that meander along the level sand of the Pine Barrens to the south.

The trail (now with a red-green blaze) swings over a small footbridge and leads past a moist hollow which is filled with ferns. Christmas fern, cinnamon fern, and spinulose woodfern are among the ferns that thrive in the protection of this gradual north-facing slope. The trail then reaches a knoll that is obviously drier than the area traversed so far: chestnut oaks and scattered pitch pines predominate on this knoll, with a layer of drought-tolerant shrubs such as huckleberry and blueberry below.

The trail passes over a series of small creeks, each one flanked by moisture-loving shrubs and trees, and then climbs up a series of steps to reach another dry knoll. A short distance further it reaches a sand road; turn right here and follow it about ¼ mile to an open area.

This area was formerly mined for clay, as is suggested by the spoil banks that can be seen scattered about. The clay here as well as that underlying Cheesequake marsh was deposited during the Cretaceous period, at a time when the sea was encroaching upon the New Jersey coastal plain. Nearby rivers then deposited their sediments into the estuaries of this advancing sea. Unlike older sedimentary deposits in New Jersey, these sediments have remained unconsolidated; that is, they have not become rock.

The clay beds here were worked principally for pottery clay during the years when New Jersey's ceramic industry, centered at Trenton, still used native clay deposits. Today, clays from outside New Jersey are used, though clay beds are still worked in nearby South Amboy and Sayreville to provide the raw material for bricks and terra cotta.

There is a good view of the marsh from here, and also of Perrine's Pond, which is off to the left. In fall, this vista is often filled with migrating hawks. Kestrels perch on the snag next to the pond, while sharp-shinned hawks chase each other over the marsh. Ospreys on their way south can occasionally be seen circling overhead, as they pause momentarily to hunt the waters of Cheesequake Creek.

One raptor which can be seen here year round is the northern harrier, or marsh hawk, which continuously skims low over the marsh in search of rodents, reptiles, and small birds. The male marsh hawk is solid gray, while the female is brownish with dark streaking below. Both sexes have a conspicuous white rump patch. The marsh hawk's most distinctive feature is its flattened facial feathers. Like the facial disc of an owl, these feathers aid the marsh hawk in locating its prey by reflecting sound toward the ears.

Follow the trail that leads to the left out to Cheesequake Creek. A mowed path leads first through tall phragmites and then out over the marsh. Closest to the brackish waters of Cheesequake Creek grows salt-marsh cordgrass, or thatch grass, with its tough, round stems and long, coarse, sharply pointed leaves. Behind it, on parts of the marsh that are only reached by high tides, the slender, delicate salt-meadow grass predominates. Farmers used to harvest this grass as salt hay for their livestock.

Here and there on the marsh can be seen shallow depressions where very different plants are growing. These depressions, called pannes, are washed by the tides infrequently and remain dry for extended periods, during which the salt water evaporates. The salt left behind creates a very saline site, and only certain specialized plants can survive under these conditions. Two or three species of glasswort or samphire are most common, all of which are identified by their succulent, jointed stems and scalelike leaves. The glassworts add a touch of color in the fall, when they turn bright red.

Another plant that is commonly found in these saline depressions is orache, identified by its mealy, gray green, trowel-shaped leaves. Orache closely resembles lambsquarters or pigweed, the weed that is so familiar to many gardeners. The two plants are both members of the goosefoot family, as are the glassworts.

The trail ends near the bleached pilings of an old dock on Cheesequake Creek. In the late 1800s, local farmers brought fruits and vegetables to these docks to be picked up by steamboats, which carried the produce to the Amboys. Nowadays, the creek supports quieter traffic: in winter, canvasback, bufflehead, and ruddy ducks float along the lower end of the creek, while in summer, great egrets, snowy egrets, and green and great blue herons stalk the banks for crabs and fish.

Another animal of the salt marsh seen occasionally is the northern diamondback terrapin, a beautiful turtle identified by its boldly patterned sculpted carapace. Each of the large scutes (scales) of the carapace has distinctive concentric grooves and ridges. The terrapin feeds on fish, crabs, and other animals which it finds in the creek. Severely reduced in number by market hunting in the late 1800s and early 1900s, the terrapin is today making a comeback.

Backtrack to the sand road, and then follow it back to the trail intersection. Turn right onto Cedar Trail, which has a green blaze. The trail soon ascends a low knoll overlooking the marsh before descending to a boardwalk which crosses a swampy area. Jewelweed, sweet pepperbush, tearthumb, and dodder form dense thickets here, providing ample cover for towhees, redwing blackbirds, phoebes, and other birds. The boardwalk envelops a red maple tree in the middle of the swamp; although it adapts to a wide variety of soil and moisture conditions, the red maple is most commonly found in damp areas like this one. Red maple is readily identified by its three-lobed, coarsely toothed leaves, its reddish, oppositely arranged twigs and buds, and by its samaras (seed cases), which are shaped like bees' wings. In early spring, sometimes while the snow is still on the ground, the red maple takes on a crimson cast from the blooming of its short clusters of small red flowers.

Beyond the boardwalk, the trail leads up a hill and then bears right before reaching another boardwalk, this one leading through an Atlantic white cedar swamp. On even the hottest summer days, these dense cedars create a cool microclimate which provides welcome relief from the blazing sun.

Bear left at the end of the boardwalk and follow the trail out to a dirt road; turn left here. Follow this road about ⅓ mile to where it intersects a green-blazed trail; turn right here and immediately bear left at the fork. The trail skirts the edge of a marsh and then passes through woods of black birch, red maple, and red and white oak. The forest floor here is carpeted with Canada mayflower, whose small white flowers dot the ground in May. Like many of the herbs of the oak forest, Canada mayflower spreads by means of underground runners.

As the trail nears a small stream, it encounters a narrow swath of bottomland trees. The huge tulip trees and an enormous sycamore here are humbling in their proportions. The trail crosses a small section of boardwalk flanked by Japanese knotweed, then enters more oak woods. After skirting the edge of a small pond, the trail winds past scattered beech and sweet gum trees before reaching another dirt road. Turn left here and follow the road past the picnic area and field, then bear right onto the green trail again.

About ⅓ mile further, the trail reaches a dirt road. Turn right here and follow this road back to the parking area.

# 18. Rancocas State Park

Distance: 2½ miles (Easy)
Walking time: 1½ hours
Directions: From Interstate 295, take exit 44A and go east on Rancocas Rd. about 1½ miles to the Rancocas Nature Center entrance (on the right). Park in the lot next to the center, which is open 9:00 A.M. to 5:00 P.M. daily except Mondays and holidays.

---

Rancocas State Park, an 1,100-acre area along the north and south branches of Rancocas Creek, is located in the physiographic region known as the Inner Coastal Plain. The Inner Coastal Plain serves as the transportation corridor for traffic between the northeast's major cities, and as such, has undergone extensive industrial, commercial, and residential development. Those areas that are not devoted to these uses have been cleared for fruit, vegetable, dairy, and poultry farming. As a result, little forested area remains in this region. Rancocas State Park, in addition to preserving extensive lowland areas, preserves an interesting array of upland forest types.

Before you begin your walk, stop at the Rancocas Nature Center, which is operated by the New Jersey Audubon Society. The center contains a small museum area, a book and gift shop, and a reference library.

From the parking lot, walk to the field beyond the barn and the shed at the end of the driveway. Two mowed trails run out into this field; take the left one. A variety of plants typical of abandoned fields grows along this trail. A surprising number of these plants are not native to this continent, but were brought here from Europe by early settlers. Some plants were introduced accidentally, but many were brought knowingly as garden herbs.

One such plant that is common in this field is Queen

126

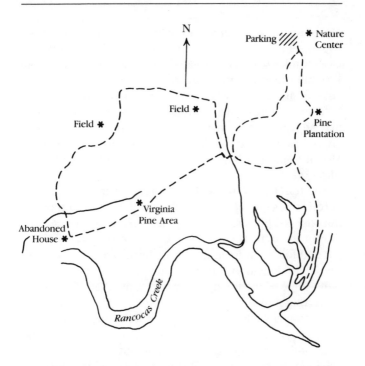

Anne's lace, also known as wild carrot, since it is a close relative of our domestic carrot. In the plant's first year, it looks just like a carrot, producing a rosette of feathery leaves, which when pulled up, will reveal a thick white taproot that looks and smells like a small carrot.

The common Saint-John's-wort is another alien plant that prospers in this field. It can be recognized by its paired leaves and stems, and by the five-petaled yellow flowers with conspicuous black dots on the margins of the petals. In England, it was customary to hang a certain yellow-blossomed plant in your window on the eve of Saint John's Day (June 24), in order to ward off evil spirits. Eventually the plant became known as Saint-John's-wort (wort meaning plant or herb).

If you look toward the east (left) as you walk along the

mowed path, you will see a low hill in the distance. This 183-foot hill is Mount Holly, a remnant of a distinctive landform known as a cuesta. The cuesta was formed about 100 million years ago, while most of South Jersey was covered by the sea, when sediments laid down on the sea bottom became cemented together to form a long rock-like ridge. Other remnants trace the outline of this now-eroded ridge—the Highlands of the Navesink and Arney's Mount to the north, and Mount Laurel and Mullica Hill to the south.

The trail leaves the field and enters a plantation of coniferous trees, including our native white pine and three introduced species: Austrian pine, Norway spruce, and European larch. The trail then forks (near stake 11); bear left and follow it down the slope through a forest of oaks, holly, and dogwood. Further along, the trail reaches the outer edge of the floodplain, where a number of trees preferring moister soil are found: red maple, river birch, sour gum, and the conspicuous umbrella magnolia. Its large (eighteen-inch) dark green leaves crowded near the ends of the branches give this truly southern tree a tropical appearance. The umbrella magnolia's showy white flowers appear in May, and these give way to interesting-looking large brownish conelike fruit clusters in September.

The trail skirts a branch of Rancocas Creek for a short distance and then comes to a dead end at a backwater marsh of the creek. This spot offers a view of an extensive stand of wild rice, which thrives in the silty muck along the Rancocas. The rodlike seeds of this tall, plume-topped grass are a favorite food of a variety of ducks, among them pintail, blue-winged teal, and ring-necked, all of which can be seen here in the spring.

Another plant growing in this marsh, which is relished by many birds, is smartweed, of which there are half a dozen different species. All are recognized by their tight,

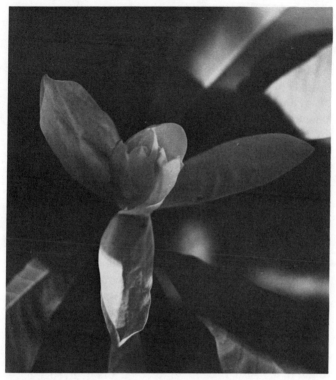

Umbrella magnolia, Rancocas State Park

spikelike clusters of tiny pink or whitish flowers and "knotted" stems with a papery sheath at each joint. Along with the many ducks a number of familiar songbirds—cardinals, redwing blackbirds, fox sparrows, song sparrows, and swamp sparrows—feed on smartweed seeds.

Backtrack to the point where you left the main trail, then bear left to follow this trail again. It winds through woods of sweet gum, black oak, and scattered tulip trees before reaching a huge sycamore tree. A short distance further (just beyond marker 18), look for a trail leading to the left; follow this trail down the hill and across a small creek, then turn right. The trail comes to another junction almost immediately; bear left here. This sandy footpath leads past oaks, American beech, and stands of mountain laurel. About ¼ mile from the junction, it enters a stand of Virginia pine. The Virginia pine is recognized by its short, twisted needles, which grow in bundles of two. Its squat appearance as a young tree and the fact that it rarely grows taller than forty to fifty feet combine to give this tree the alternative name of scrub pine. This stand of Virginia pine will yield eventually to deciduous forest like the type passed through earlier, since although it is an aggressive colonizer of abandoned fields, it cannot compete effectively in the long run with the broad-leaved trees.

Another ⅛ mile further, the trail comes out to an old blacktop road which leads to an abandoned house. Turn right and follow this road over a creek, up a hill, and past another building. The trail then comes out into an open area; bear right here and follow the edge of the field. Along this section of the trail you may occasionally see a small brownish creature streak across the sand and up a nearby tree. This is the northern fence lizard, also known as the pine lizard, because of its frequent occurrence in open pine woods.

The trail reenters the woods and then shortly passes into another open field. Follow along the edge of this field to where the trail enters the woods once more, then follow a few hundred yards to where you crossed the creek earlier. Bear left across the creek and return to the marked nature trail. The trial passes through more upland woods before reaching another field.

Just before the trail reaches the parking area, it passes a large tree with black, checkered bark and glossy egg-shaped leaves. This is a persimmon tree, most easily recognized in the fall, when its small pumpkin-colored fruits dot the tree. The sweet, pulpy fruits, when ripe, are favored by deer, raccoons, and opossums, as well as people. Don't try tasting the green fruit though, or you'll really pucker up.

# The Pine Barrens

Cranberry harvester, Lebanon State Park

# 19. Lebanon State Forest

*Pakim Pond Area*
Distance: 5 miles (Moderate)
Walking time: 2½ hours
Directions: Take NJ 70 to NJ 72, then go southeast on NJ 72 for 3 miles. Look for a sign saying Pakim Pond, and turn left and follow ¾ mile to parking area. A parking fee is charged for day use between Memorial Day and Labor Day.

The New Jersey Pine Barrens have always attracted attention because of the region's rich human and natural history; their precarious position today as a vast forest wilderness in the midst of the nation's most densely populated state has increased their appeal. Comprising some 2,000 square miles, the area is the most extensive tract of wildland in the northeast.

Though the flat, sandy expanses of pitch pine which give the region its name are the typical image of the Pine Barrens, the most noteworthy natural features are the wet lowland swamps and bogs that crisscross the region. This walk takes in a typical pitch pine barrens, as well as some interesting lowland communities.

From the parking lot, walk through the picnic area near Pakim Pond, and look for a white-blazed trail which leads left to a sand road. Bear right onto this sand road and follow it for about a mile. The forest here is typical pitch pine lowland forest, made up almost entirely of pitch pine, whose irregularly arranged branches, scaly bark, and gnarled trunk distinguish it from other pines found in New Jersey. Black, blackjack, and post oaks are occasionally scattered among the pines. Two other oaks are seen in the understory: the scrub oak (also called bear oak) and less commonly, the dwarf chinquapin (or dwarf

134

Cranberry Bogs

Reservoir

Reservoir

✳ Abandoned
Blueberry Bog

Cedar Swamp
✳

N
↑

Pakim Pond

Parking

chestnut) oak. Both of their names are descriptive of their size; neither of these trees usually grows more than ten feet tall. The scrub oak has oblong leaves with five to seven pointed lobes separated by shallow sinuses, and twigs that are covered with short brown fuzz. The dwarf chestnut oak has leaves like those of the chestnut oak, but they are smaller and have fewer teeth.

Shared by all of these trees is an ability to withstand the extreme dryness of the sandy soil. Even though the region's annual precipitation is over forty inches, rainfall drains so rapidly through the porous sands that the water is largely unavailable to plants at the surface. This droughtiness makes for an extremely flammable forest,

and fires of huge proportions are an almost annual oc-
curence in the Pine Barrens. The pitch pine is one of only
three pines in the United States that responds to fire by
sending forth sprouts, and invariably while walking one
comes across pines with green crowns that have trunks
still blackened by fire. The pitch pine not only tolerates
fire, but is favored by it, since periodic blazes destroy the
litter that accumulates on the forest floor. In time, this
litter would prevent the establishment of young pine
seedlings, eventually leading to an oak-dominated forest.

The sand road comes to a junction where it meets a
narrower sand road; turn right here. Almost immediately
a number of trees appear that hint there is water nearby:
red maple, gray birch, sweet bay, sassafras, and sweet pepperbush. The first white cedars appear also, and shortly
the road crosses Cooper Branch, one of three streams that
join at Presidential Lakes before continuing west to empty
into the Rancocas River. Another 250 yards further, the
road forks; bear left onto another sand road.

The swamp forest disappears as quickly as it appeared,
and again the trail leads through dry pine woods. The
shrubs growing here are as well adapted to drought and
fire as are the trees; sheep laurel and bracken fern, the
most common shrubs, are especially vigorous after a fire.
Sheep laurel, a close relative of the familiar mountain laurel, has small leathery, evergreen leaves which are pale
green below.

The road passes a semiopen area on the right; this is a
small blueberry plantation which has been abandoned for
some time. The mounded rows of plants can still be seen,
and in the fall a handful of berries can usually be harvested. It was at Whitesbog, just a few miles to the north,
that the cultivated blueberry was developed by Elizabeth
White in the early 1900s. In and around the Pine Barrens
there are about 10,000 acres devoted to cultivated blueberry production, making New Jersey the nation's num-
ber-one producer of this crop.

Beyond the blueberry field the road forks; stay right. Immediately the road passes out of the woods to follow the edge of a large pond. In dry years the stumps of hundreds of white cedar trees stick up out of the mud, revealing that the pond is actually a cedar swamp that was cut over and flooded to serve as a reservoir. To the left of the road is a row of silver-barked hawthorn trees, and beyond it a young red cedar woodland which has developed on an abandoned cranberry bog.

Follow the trail along the edge of the pond until it passes back into the woods. Red-bellied and painted turtles slip from their pondside basking places into the tea-colored water as you walk past, and ducks and geese are commonly seen feeding further out. In summers when the reservoir is dry, herons step cautiously amid the cedar stumps, patiently searching the mud for their prey. Most common is the strikingly colored green heron. This small, dark heron has bright orange legs, a chestnut head and neck, a black crown, and a dark green back and wings.

After passing through woods for about ¼ mile, the road comes to a junction. Bear left and follow the road between two dormant cranberry bogs for a few hundred yards before turning right onto another sand road. This road passes a turnoff to the left, then comes to a T; bear right at this intersection and then immediately bear left. This circuitous route has finally brought you to an active cranberry bog. Like the reservoir seen earlier, this bog was originally a white-cedar swamp probably cut over in the late nineteenth century and perhaps excavated for bog iron. It was this activity that led to the beginning of commercial cranberrying in the 1860s, when such bogs were turfed out by hand. Low dams like these were then built from the turf, after which wild cranberries from alongside nearby streams were transplanted into them. The bogs are flooded in autumn to permit harvest, and to keep cold winter winds from drying out the vines.

In the early days, cranberries were harvested by hand

with many-tiered wooden scoops that pickers swung through the vines like large claws. Today, mechanical harvesting equipment has replaced the laborious hand methods of the past, and in summer or fall, one or more of the odd-looking harvesting machines can usually be seen resting alongside one of the dams.

Turn left where the road meets another intersection, and follow this for a few hundred yards through pine woods until it meets the intersection of two roads. Take the middle road, which leads along another shallow reservoir, and follow this past the reservoir and back into the woods. From here, follow this road ¼ mile to where it meets a larger sand road and turn left.

Occasionally while walking this road, you may run across one of the Pine Barrens' most distinctive animals, the northern pine snake. This large black and white snake spends much of its time burrowing in the soft sands, but sometimes moves about above ground. When disturbed, the pine snake makes itself conspicuous—striking out with its head, hissing loudly, and vibrating its tail. The entire display is convincing, yet there is little to fear, as the pine snake is not venomous.

The pine snake is one of three burrowing snakes whose distribution in New Jersey is limited almost exclusively to the soft sand of the Pine Barrens. The other two are the corn snake and the scarlet snake. The corn snake, the larger of the two, has a red or orange body which, in cross section, is shaped something like a slice of bread; that is, it has a distinctly flat belly, which meets the sides of its body at an angle. The third, the scarlet snake, is one of New Jersey's most beautiful snakes; it has a red head, and its more-rounded body is crossed by red saddles bordered by black.

The road reaches the junction where earlier you turned right to reach the cranberry bogs; turn right to follow the overgrown sand road for about ½ mile and then bear left at the fork. Here the road skirts the edge of a cedar swamp, as can be seen from the red maples, young white cedars, and damp soil. In spring and summer this is a good place to listen for the loud, clear "tawee-tawee-tawee-tee-o" song of the hooded warbler. The male hooded warbler is one of the handsomest of the wood warbler family, with a bright yellow face and jet black hood. A number of other warblers nest in cedar and hardwood swamps throughout the New Jersey coastal plain; the black and white, black-throated green, and prothonotary warblers are among the most common.

Follow the road ¾ mile through more pine woods, passing the white-blazed Batona Trail along the way. This 39-mile trail was built by the Batona Hiking Club of Philadelphia in 1961. The road leads back to the sand road you began on, and after turning right onto this road, it is only a short walk back to the parking area.

# 20. Wharton State Forest

*Batsto Village Area*
Distance: 3 miles (Moderate)
Walking time: 3 hours
Directions: Take the Garden State Parkway to exit 49. Go
west on County Rd. 542 about 12 miles, then turn right at
sign marking Batsto Historic Area. Park in the lot across
from the visitor's center. A parking fee is charged during
the summer.

One hundred and fifty years ago, Batsto was a dirty industrial village where the blast furnace roared incessantly,
smoke filled the air, and water-powered mills turned out
cornmeal and sawed boards to serve the needs of the
town's 900 inhabitants. Today, Batsto is a quiet restored
village where the gristmill grinds corn for sale to visitors,
and the sawmill cuts white cedar shingles for use in the
restoration of Batsto's buildings. The Wharton State Forest
headquarters are located here, and were it not for this
fact, Batsto would have become one of the Pine Barrens'
many vanished towns.

The story of Batsto begins in 1766, when Charles Read
erected the Batsto Furnace and began producing kettles,
skillets, stoves, and a variety of other iron products. In
1770, Col. John Cox, assistant quartermaster general of
the Continental Army, acquired control of the ironworks,
and began casting cannon and cannonballs for use against
the British during the Revolutionary War. Later, the furnace would also furnish munitions for the War of 1812,
water pipe for New York City, and the steam cylinder for
one of John Fitch's experimental steamboats.

Competition from Pennsylvania furnaces using easier to
obtain mineral ore eventually forced the Batsto Furnace

to close in 1848, but as the iron industry died, a new one
was born—glass manufacturing. Using the white Pine Barrens' sand as its principal raw material, the Batsto glass-
works produced flat glass for windows and street lamps.
Many of the gas lamps that lighted the streets of New York
and Philadelphia during the latter part of the nineteenth
century contained Batsto glass.

Begin your walk with a tour of Batsto; a trail map which
identifies the various buildings in the village can be obtained at the visitor's center. Batsto Furnace and the glass-
works are no longer standing, but as you walk through
the village, you will see signs of their former presence.
Half-buried in the sand are fragments of seashells brought
here from the coast for use as flux in the furnace. The
shells were introduced to purify the iron, as the calcium
carbonate in them combined with impurities to form a
slag which floated on top of the molten iron. Pieces of
this slag can also be seen scattered about, and thousands
of pieces of glass, in hues of green, blue, and amber, attest
to the previous existence of the glass factory.

To begin the trail walk, follow the road that leads to
the Nature Center. Just beyond the center, where the road
bends to the right, there is a trail on the left-hand side;
begin here. At the entrance to the trail are some large
pieces of bog iron, which was the type of iron ore used
at the Batsto Furnace.

Bog iron is formed when rainwater that has leached

iron from the sands moves underground into nearby streams and then oxidizes on contact with the air. The oxidized iron forms a rusty-colored scum on the surface which drifts over to the bank of the stream, where it permeates the sands and gravels to such an extent that it forms an iron-sandstone composite like the rocks here. Batsto ore raisers would skim the bog iron from the surface of streams or dig it from the banks, then haul it overland to the furnace in wagons or by water in long, flat-bottomed ore boats.

The trail enters a stretch of typical Pine Barrens woods—pitch pine and black oak with a lower layer of blueberry, huckleberry, and sheep laurel shrubs—and continues a short distance before reaching the junction of two marked trails. Take the left trail, which has a yellow over red blaze. To the right of the trail here are several sweet bay magnolias which mark the edge of a small cedar swamp. The sweet bay is a small tree with thick, leathery, elliptic leaves which smell spicy when crushed. Wherever the sweet bay is seen in the Pine Barrens, it is certain that there is ample water nearby. Along this trail it often grows beside the small streams that run down into Batsto Lake.

Another ¼ mile further the trail forks again; follow the left-hand trail, which is marked by a yellow blaze. This trail continues to provide beautiful views upstream toward the northern end of Batsto Lake, which is usually full even in times of prolonged drought. This is because the enormous volume of groundwater beneath the sandy soil continually recharges the surface stream, ponds, and bogs of the Pine Barrens.

The water in Batsto Lake, and in most of the rivers and lakes of the Pine Barrens, is a dark tea color. This is caused by the combination of tannins leached from nearby cedar trees and iron from the groundwater. Despite its unappealing color, Pine Barrens water is remarkably pure. A century ago, sea captains took Pine Barrens "cedar wa-

Joseph Wharton mansion, Batsto Village

ter" with them on voyages, since it would remain sweet longer than any other water available to them.

Along certain sections of this trail are two shrubs that are typical of lowland areas in the Pine Barrens: sweet pepperbush and fetterbush, or swamp sweetbells. Both of these shrubs have thin, fine-toothed leaves; however, those of the sweet pepperbush are short pointed and those of the fetterbush long pointed. Sweet pepperbush is also distinguished by its hairy twigs, which are held erect, and by the fact that it often occurs in colonies, as it is one of the few shrubs that may reproduce by means of underground runners. Both plants have very fragrant flowers, the fetterbush blooming in mid-May, the sweet pepperbush in late summer.

Another plant seen along this part of the trail is turkeybeard. A member of the lily family, turkeybeard is identified by its tall stalk supporting a cluster of white flowers that arise from a tussock of long, grasslike leaves. Turkeybeard is unusual in that its range is largely restricted to mountain woods of the southern Appalachians, yet it emerges onto the Coastal Plain briefly in Delaware and occurs commonly here in the Pine Barrens, where it reaches its northern limit. There are over 100 other plants which, like turkeybeard, reach their northern geographic limit in the Pine Barrens. At the same time, there are at least 21 species of northern plants that reach their southern limit here, making the Pine Barrens the region with the greatest overlap in plant ranges of eastern North America.

The trail eventually swings away from the water's edge and leads out onto a sand road. Bear left onto this road and follow it ¼ mile. The fine white sand along this road is only barely covered by vegetation in many places, mostly lichens and patches of downy hudsonia, also known as golden heather. Golden heather is a mosslike shrub which has short, needlelike leaves and small yellow flowers, which spill out over the sands in late spring.

The sand road ends and a trail enters the woods to follow the edge of the lake again. This trail eventually comes to a dead end, but it is worth following because it leads to an old beaver lodge. As you walk along the trail, you can see many signs of beaver activity. Most obvious are the numerous beaver-felled trees; if you look at the base of most of the fallen trees here, you'll see small piles of wood chips left by a gnawing beaver. Beavers cut down trees for three reasons: for food, for building their lodge and dam, and to keep their continually growing teeth worn down. Although they prefer the bark of trees like poplar, birch, and willow as food, here in the Pine Barrens they make do with scrub oak, white cedar, and pitch pine.

The trail has finally reached the upper reaches of Batsto Lake, where the pine woods begin to give way to a large white cedar swamp. Small white cedar islands can be seen to the left of the trail, and it is on the edge of one of these islands that the beavers have built their lodge. As the trail skirts the edge of the water, another indication of beaver activity can be seen: here a trail used repeatedly by the beavers leads into the lake.

Continue on the trail just up the hill beyond this beaver path and look to the left. The low conical lodge built of sticks and mud can be seen on the opposite bank. Inside the lodge is a chamber which is connected with the outside by a number of tunnels that open underwater. In winter, the beavers store saplings under the water near the lodge, and they can leave the lodge via these tunnels and return to their chamber with some of the saplings for food.

From here, return via the same trail to the sand road. Early in the evenings beginning in late April one can hear carpenter frogs calling from the sedge hummocks along the edge of the lake. The carpenter frog gets its name from its call, which sounds like two carpenters hitting nails one right after the other. Large choruses sound like a whole construction crew hammering away.

Though easily heard, the carpenter frog is harder to see, as it is only about two inches long, and its brownish color blends perfectly with the tannin-stained water. Its occurrence in the Pine Barrens is interesting, since it is at its northern limit here, and yet it often outnumbers more widely distributed frogs such as the spring peeper, chorus frog, and wood frog. This is because the carpenter frog has adapted to the extremely acidic water of the Pine Barrens' streams and bogs. Its eggs, and also those of the lovely Pine Barrens tree frog, can survive in water where the pH is as low as 4.0 (7.0 is neutral).

When you reach the sand road again, follow it to where you first joined it and then bear left. Follow this road about ¼ mile until it meets another sand road and then bear right. The woods here are dominated by black oak rather than pitch pine, although the pitch pine is still common, and they are somewhat sparser than the pine forest traveled through earlier.

It is hard to tell today, but all of these forests have been cut repeatedly to produce charcoal which fueled the fires of the Batsto Furnace. To make charcoal, colliers—as the men who made charcoal were called—stacked cordwood cut from the nearby forest into ten- to twenty-foot-high vertical stacks and then covered the wood with pieces of sandy turf. This turf covering kept the wood from burning too quickly by cutting off the supply of oxygen to the fire. The colliers dropped burning kindling into a hole in the top of the mound and sealed it over. They kept watch over it day and night for a week or more, carefully regulating the air supply by opening and closing vents in the mound, until the wood was evenly charred. Finally, carters hauled the charcoal by wagon to the furnace, whose roar they could most likely hear as they came over the sand roads.

After about ¾ mile, the road reaches a junction marked by a wooden fence on the right. The sand here is littered with refuse from Batsto's earlier days: slag, charcoal, pieces of bog iron, and even scraps of finished iron. Turn right onto the paved road and follow it back to Batsto Village.

# The Atlantic Coast

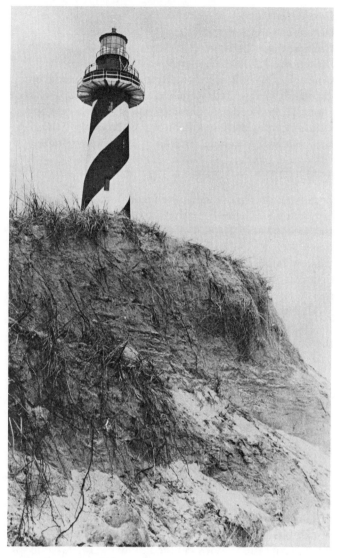

Lighthouse, Atlantic coast
*Courtesy Rick Zeroka*

# 21. Gateway National Recreation Area

*Sandy Hook*
Distance: 5 miles (Moderate)
Walking time: 2½ hours
Directions: Take the Garden State Parkway to exit 117.
Go east on NJ 36 toward Highlands. After crossing the
Highlands bridge, bear right and follow signs to park
entrance. Proceed past entrance and go 2 miles to the
visitor's center parking lot (on right). To explore the Fort
Hancock area, you must pick up a "History Pass" here.

---

Because it dominates a major channel into New York harbor, Sandy Hook has been the site of lighthouses, forts,
and weapons emplacements since the earliest of colonial
times. As early as 1687, Sandy Hook was considered extremely important to the defense of New York City. In
that year, the royal governor of New York offered a plan
that would "make up a small Fort with twelve guns upon
Sandy Hook, the channel there being so near the shore
that no vessel can go in or out but she must come so near
the Point that from on board ship one might toss a biscuit
cake on shore."

Sandy Hook's uniqueness lies not only in its rich history, but also in its natural environment of holly forests,
fresh- and saltwater marshes, sand dunes, and scores of
migrating birds. As with most of the shore walks described in this book, this one is more enjoyable in the fall
or early spring, when hot weather, mosquitoes, and
crowds can be avoided.

You may wish to stop at the Spermaceti Cove Visitor's
Center before you begin your walk. The building, which
originally served as a lifesaving station, houses a variety
of exhibits on the history and natural history of Sandy
Hook. From the visitor's center, follow the road that loops

around the center and look for the "Old Dune Trail" sign on the right. This trail weaves through the backdune area, which has been stabilized by the growth of various plants. At the entrance to the trail some of these plants can be seen: poison ivy, seaside goldenrod, beach heather, and bayberry. Found here, though less common elsewhere on the dunes, is the groundsel-tree. Actually a shrub, the groundsel-tree is recognized by its small white silky flowers and fruits and its thick gray green leaves. These leaves can be confusing, as those on the upper part of the plant are small and often lack teeth, while those on the lower part are larger and wedge shaped, and have large teeth. The groundsel-tree is more commonly found in the upper margins of coastal salt marshes.

Though small and usually hugging the sand, the prickly pear cactus growing here is hard to overlook. In summer it boasts showy yellow flowers, and these give way to purplish red fruits in the fall. These pulpy fruits are edible, but be sure to remove the spines first. Covering the thick, fleshy skins as well as the fruits, these spines are actually modified leaves which protect the plant from herbivorous animals. The spines do not keep all animals away, however, and many prickly pear cacti can be found with teeth marks along the stem. This is the work of the cottontail rabbit who obtains water from the succulent stem.

*Gateway National Recreation Area* 149

After crossing a small road, the trail comes to a grove of holly trees. This grove is actually part of the large holly forest that covers much of the bay side of this portion of Sandy Hook. This is the most extensive stand of American holly along the Atlantic coast and has been set aside as a natural area for scientific research. Many of the trees in the natural area are over 100 years old, and the oldest is over 300 years.

After emerging from the holly grove, you pass many bleached red cedar snags—standing dead trees from which most of the leaves and limbs have fallen. These have been killed by salt spray, which limits the growth of all the trees close to the ocean beach. It has been found that plant growth is limited to a level below a fifteen-degree line drawn from the water's edge; this level is known as the salt-spray horizon.

The trail passes an old dirt road and a sign warning of possible live artillery shells in the dunes. From 1874 to 1919, all testing of army guns took place at the Sandy Hook Proving Ground, and although an extensive search has been conducted, the possibility exists that some live shells are still here. Many of these old roads date back to that era, when they linked together an extensive ammunition storage complex.

The trail then comes upon a small freshwater pond. This pond actually began as a saltwater lagoon which became separated from the salt water of ocean and bay by shifting sands. Over the years rainfall has formed a layer of fresh water on top of the salt water that remained in the pond. Since fresh water is not as heavy as salt water, they do not mix, and an important freshwater habitat was created. Here painted turtles, green frogs, ducks, and marsh hawks have a home in an otherwise dry and forbidding landscape.

As the trail begins to curve around, it passes a former Nike-Hercules missile site. The once electrified fence surrounding the site now serves as a perch for scores of

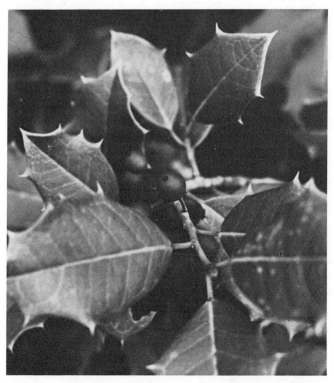

American holly, Gateway National Recreation Area

migrating songbirds in the spring and fall. Because it is located along the Atlantic flyway, the major path of bird migration in the eastern United States, a wide variety of migrants can be seen at Sandy Hook. The birds tend to concentrate along Sandy Hook before and after crossing the open-water expanse of New York Bay. Most numerous are myrtle warblers, which can be seen foraging for the berries of bayberry, red cedar, and poison ivy. Though the fall and spring migrations bring as many as twenty or more species of warbler to Sandy Hook, the myrtle is easily recognized, as it is the only yellow-rumped warbler with a white throat.

The trail curves back around to join the dirt road again; follow it away from the beach out to the main road. Turn right and follow this road for about ¾ mile. The road partially follows the old bed of the New Jersey Southern Railroad, which once extended to the northern tip of Horseshoe Cove, where there was a steamboat landing. In fall, one often finds exhausted monarch butterflies along the side of the road. Monarchs follow much the same path as migrating birds and are often seen on Sandy Hook. You may also see an occasional box turtle along the road here.

After passing the turnoff to North Beach, the road comes to the Halyburton Monument, which was erected in memory of Lieut. Hamilton Douglas-Halyburton. Shortly after the Revolutionary War had ended, the ships of the Royal Navy were at anchor in Sandy Hook Bay while waiting to evacuate the British army from New York City. While anchored there, a small group of seamen deserted one of the ships, the HMS *Assistance*. Lieutenant Halyburton and thirteen members of his crew went after them in a small boat, but were caught in a sudden blizzard. Halyburton and his men were later found frozen to death and were buried somewhere on Sandy Hook. A monument was erected but was destroyed by vandals, and the site was lost until 1908 when railroad workers digging for the new railroad line uncovered the old burial vault. This monument was erected then.

As you pass the salt marsh on Horseshoe Cove, look out to the northern point of the cove. This is one of the barbs that make Sandy Hook such a distinctive landform. When viewed on a map, South Island and the northern tip of Spermaceti Cove similarly appear as barbs, while the tip of the sand spit forms the hook. These formations are clues to the geologic processes that have created Sandy Hook.

Sandy Hook began as a small sandbar formed from shell fragments and sediments. The alongshore current, moving north along the coast, deposited more sand on the bar until it became an island. Too weak to maintain a continuous line, the current that produced the island swung westward into an embayment, thus forming a hook (South Island). Sea Bright, the barrier beach to the south of the island, extended northward via the same process to connect with the hook, forming what geologists call a sand spit. With the shallowing of the water by the growth of the spit, the current gradually resumed its straight course until it again turned inward to form a second barb—Spermaceti Cove. The process repeated itself again to form Horseshoe Cove, and it is only periodic dredging that has prevented Sandy Hook from growing in this manner out into the shipping channel leading to New York City.

Another ⅛ mile further, where the road forks, bear right and follow the road to the entrance to Fort Hancock. Fort Hancock and its gun batteries were constructed during the 1890s to protect the entrance to New York harbor. Once a bustling army town of hundreds of officers, enlisted men, and their families, Fort Hancock is now a strange ghost town. Barracks, mess halls, and other buildings stand empty, and grass grows up out of the brick paths.

Enter the parade ground, which is flanked by enlisted men's barracks on the right and officers' quarters on the left. The officers' quarters, which appear to be a bit neglected now, were stately homes built for the married officers of the coast artillery. The largest house, in the middle of the row, was the commanding officer's. In the summer, the houses are used by nonprofit organizations such as scouting groups and community centers.

At the end of the parade ground, turn right and follow the road to the guard house, which now serves as the Sandy Hook Museum. A variety of historic photographs and artifacts are exhibited here, some housed in the original jail cells. From the museum, head for the lighthouse, which can be seen just a short distance away.

Constructed by the colony of New York to reduce shipping losses on the outer shoals of Sandy Hook, Sandy Hook lighthouse is the oldest lighthouse in the United States and has been in operation since 1764. Though originally built only 500 feet from the end of the hook, the lighthouse today is about one and one-half miles away, because the end of the sand spit has been built up by alongshore currents.

From the lighthouse, follow the road toward the beach to the Battery Gunnison, a massive concrete artillery battery which was erected in 1904. Although the guns are gone, the surrounding parapets, the tunnels connecting the cartridge rooms, and the mechanical cartridge-lifting machines can still be seen. From the battery there is an excellent view of the Manhattan skyline and the rest of New York City.

To return, you may wish to walk along the beach; however, a large portion is closed during the summer to protect nesting shorebirds. The other route is to walk back to the road, turn left, and follow the road back to the visitor's center.

# 22. Island Beach State Park

Distance: 5 miles (Moderate)
Walking time: 2½ hours
Directions: Take the Garden State Parkway to exit 82.
Then take NJ 37 east to NJ 35 south. Go past park en-
trance and continue to parking lot A-8. The parking fee is
$4.00 on weekends in summer, $3.00 on weekdays, and
$1.00 off season.

As one of the last natural expanses of barrier beach along
the Atlantic shore, Island Beach State Park is truly worth a
visit. While all of New Jersey's other barrier islands have
undergone extensive development, this ten-mile strip remains in its natural state. It is a fragile strip which owes
its existence to the ocean, and yet the ocean constantly
threatens to destroy it.

Because most of the park has been set aside as a botani-
cal preserve, there are no extensive trails. An interesting
walk can, however, be created by walking the series of
trails that lead from the road out to the ocean beaches.
Because these beaches are flooded with people during the
summer, this walk is best if taken after Labor Day. (The
parking fee is reduced then also.)

From parking lot A-8, follow the path that leads to the
beach. Immediately you enter a thicket of low-growing
shrubs and trees. The most obvious plant is American
holly, joined by wild cherry and shadbush. Almost as soon
as you have entered this thicket, you leave it behind, and
come to the top of the foredune, the dune closest to the
beach. From here you can see the ocean in front of you
and still look back to see Barnegat Bay behind.

There is a noticeable increase in the force of the wind
as one climbs to the top of the dune, and it is the wind
that is responsible for much of the lay of the land of the

ATLANTIC OCEAN

A-8
Parking
A-9    A-10    A-11    A-12    A-13
Marsh *

Barnegat Bay

⟶ N

barrier beach. The wind picks up sand from the beach and deposits it on the dunes behind. Over time, a series of dunes like the ones visible from this rise is created.

As you continue toward the beach, the vegetation becomes sparse, consisting mainly of beach grass (also called dune grass or marram grass). Beach grass is the anchor that holds the dunes against the effects of wind and wave. Each plant has horizontal stems that creep along the sand, sending up new tufts of leaves and roots every few inches. This network of roots help to bind the sand in place, stabilizing the dune and building it higher.

In order to grow here, the beach grass must be able to survive the salt spray the wind carries with it. Only a very few plants are as tolerant of the salt spray as the beach grass, and these can be found in smaller numbers along the trail here. Most noticeable is the seaside goldenrod, with its narrow, fleshy leaves and yellow blossoms arranged in a graceful plume. If you look closely, you can see that the succulent leaves are protected by a waxy coating which helps the plant conserve moisture. Less conspicuous is the dusty miller, a low, matted plant with deeply lobed leaves that are covered with white hairs. These hairs reflect the strong sun and also provide the leaves with vital insulation from the wind and salt spray.

Continue out to the beach and turn right. In the fall, when the bluefish are running, fishermen are lined up along this beach. About 400 yards up the beach, turn right to follow the path to the next parking area. After passing the foredune again, you come to an area where the dunes have been broken by the wind into a jumble of low dunes, hollows, and broad flat swales. This area is known as the primary backdune.

Beyond the backdune area you enter a shrub thicket again. On either side of the trail can be seen the layer of leaf litter that has been built upon the top of the sand. It may seem strange that the wild cherry and American holly trees here are only growing to the same height as the blueberry and bayberry bushes. This is because the salt spray is carried back this far and kills any growth above the level of the windstream that crosses the barrier island.

After the trail emerges at parking lot A-9, turn left to follow the road. This stretch of hard ground is a relief from the soft sands of the beach and dunes. You may notice that plants found closer to the beach are also found along this road, but that they grow taller here. This is because the road lies just beyond the reach of the harshest winds and salt spray. Conditions are even less harsh on the bay side of the road, where the dunes support patches of woodland made up of red cedars, holly, wild cherry, pitch pine, and a few other trees.

Just before you reach the next parking area, you pass on the left a holly tree laden with red berries. In holly trees, the male and female flowers occur on separate trees, and only the female trees, like this one, bear fruit. The berries can be found on female trees in almost every month of the year, and thus are an important source of food for many birds.

Another holly marks the beginning of the trail from parking lot A-10. Though the trunk of this tree is only about eight inches in diameter, the tree may be as much as 120 years old. Continue toward the beach, where before reaching the foredune, the trail passes a large patch of Virginia creeper sprawled across the sand. This plant is easily recognized by its compound leaves consisting of

Seaside goldenrod, Island Beach State Park

five leaflets arranged like spokes of a wheel. In the fall, these leaves turn to crimson, and with its blue fruits, the Virginia creeper becomes one of the most colorful plants on the dunes.

Many of the low backdunes along here are covered with hudsonia, or beach heather. Because it is not very tolerant of salt spray, the beach heather tends to grow behind the foredunes in areas that are too dry to support the growth of larger plants. Its small yellow flowers dot the sands in early summer.

Again, the trail leaves the shelter of the backdunes and emerges into the foredune area. Where the trail reaches the top of the foredune, stop for a moment to look out over a sea of beach grass. At certain times in the fall, you can stand and watch as wave upon wave of migrating tree swallows skim the top of the grass. As many as a thousand or more may pass as you stand, their iridescent green backs and white bellies flashing in the sun as they go by.

After the trail emerges onto the beach again, turn right. Note that sections of the drift fence along the front of the foredune have been buried by sand carried off the beach by the wind. With so much sand constantly being taken from the beach, why does it remain?

New sand is constantly being added to the beach, deposited by the alongshore currents which sweep southward. The sand being deposited here is coming from around Long Branch and Asbury, where coastal bluffs are being severely eroded by the ocean waves. The quantity of sand carried by the alongshore currents diminishes southward, so that New Jersey's southernmost barrier beaches are much smaller and more broken up than those to the north, like Island Beach.

Leave the beach along the trail to parking lot A-11; this trail is marked by a sign and a huge blow-out—an area where the dune has largely disappeared. Although small blow-outs occur fairly often during fierce storms, they are repaired as vegetation quickly colonizes the blow-out and begins again the process of dune building. This one, however, has probably been aggravated by constant walking along the path, as the plants necessary to rebuild the dune cannot get a footing because of the trampling. This is why it is so important to stay off the dunes and remain on the designated trails.

After emerging at lot A-11, turn left along the road, which is flanked on the right by an impenetrable thicket of greenbrier. Most people have had at least one unpleasant encounter with this prickly vine. When viewed from this safe distance in the fall, the greenbrier thicket is a colorful jumble of yellow leaves and green stems. Another colorful plant along the road is dwarf or winged sumac, which has fire-red leaves in autumn. In other seasons, winged sumac is easily recognized by its large leaves which are divided into eleven to twenty-three narrow, shining leaflets. The main vein of the leaves, called the midrib, gives the shrub its name, as it is bordered by thin wings.

At parking lot A-12, follow the path once more to the beach, then turn right again and continue to the next path back through the dunes. Before reaching the road, the trail comes upon a distinctly different area. The tall feathery plumes of phragmites or reed grass are most noticeable, along with scattered red maple trees. At first, both seem out of place in this arid environment. Further along, the trail reveals that you have come upon a freshwater marsh. Along the short section of boardwalk can be seen marsh fern, royal fern, and even sphagnum moss when the water level is low. This marsh is a low-lying area that exposes the underlying groundwater table of Island Beach, which lies well below the surface in most sections of the barrier island.

Just beyond the boardwalk, the trail emerges at parking area A-13. From here, you may turn right and return via the road, or if your legs are up to it, walk out to the beach and walk by the water.

160  *Island Beach State Park*

# 23. Brigantine National Wildlife Refuge

Distance: 8 miles (Moderate)
Walking time: 4 hours
Directions: Take the Garden State Parkway to exit 48,
then go south on US 9 for 6 miles to Oceanville. Look for
the sign on the right-hand side of the road, which marks
the refuge entrance to the left. Follow the road to the
refuge headquarters and park there.

Walking the auto tour at Brigantine National Wildlife Refuge might at first seem crazy—the eight-mile loop is
along a level dirt road often crowded with cars. However,
the spectacle of tens of thousands of geese and ducks
continuously moving back and forth across the sky completely diverts one's attention from the activity on the
ground. Also, if you begin at dawn, when the refuge
opens, you will only have to share the road with a few
hardy birdwatchers.

The refuge, which consists of 20,000 acres of tidal
marsh, freshwater pools, and saltwater bays and channels,
was established in 1939 for the protection and manage-
ment of migratory waterfowl. The area is a major stopping
point along the Atlantic flyway, as well as being an important wintering area for as many as 150,000 geese, ducks,
and other birds. Except for summer, when mosquitoes
and greenhead flies are biting, Brigantine National Wildlife
Refuge is a spectacular place to visit year round. March
and April and October and November bring the great
waterfowl migrations, but a variety of other birds can be
seen in the remaining months. In January and February,
especially during a warm spell, one can see diving ducks,
rough-legged hawks, short-eared owls, and occasionally, a
bald eagle or snowy owl. The beautiful glossy ibis is abun-

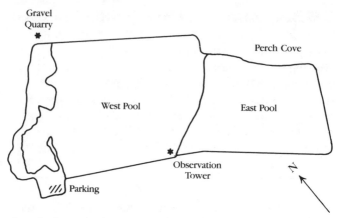

dant in late April, and August heralds the gathering of large numbers of shorebirds and waders.

Follow the auto road past the gate, down around a grassy field, and then turn right onto the main dike. To the left is West Pool, a 900-acre largely freshwater pool. Water control devices along the dike prevent the entrance of salt water from the bay, while allowing fresh water to flow out. The water level in this pool is regulated by refuge managers in order to control plant growth, and to make aquatic foods available to various types of waterfowl.

To the right of you as you walk is an extensive area of salt marsh. Here silt and nutrients from upland runoff were deposited, then stabilized by plants that can tolerate periodic inundation by salt water. The carpetlike plant growing above the high tide line is salt-meadow grass (also called salt-marsh hay). Its weak stems tend to fall over in swirling mats, giving the appearance of grassy cowlicks. In fact, this marsh may have had cows on it at one time, since many farmers along the coast pastured their cows on the salt-meadow grass. Today the plant provides food for geese, muskrat, and meadow voles, who eat the roots as well as the stems.

The other principal plant of the salt marsh is the salt-marsh cordgrass (or thatch grass), which is taller and has stiff round stems and long, coarse, sharply pointed leaves. It can stand more wetness than the salt-meadow grass, and so is usually found growing closer to the water. It provides nesting cover for sharp-tailed and seaside sparrows, both of which also feed on its seeds.

After walking about a mile, you reach a large observation tower, which is definitely worth the climb. On late autumn afternoons, you can watch thousands of brant, Canada geese, and snow geese lift off from bays to the northeast and fly straight toward you before veering off to settle down for a drink in the pool below. The sound of so many birds on such an afternoon is awesome. From the tower also can be seen the changing colors of the marsh. The salt-marsh grasses and reeds are blue green and yellow green in the summer, tawny and gold in the fall, and dun colored in winter. In the middle of summer, the flowers of the salt-marsh hay form violet patches on the marsh.

Continue past the cross dike that separates West Pool from this area of brackish water and low islands, which is managed as a nesting area for a variety of ducks. These islands serve as nest sites, not only for the abundant mallard and black ducks, but for pintails, blue- and green-winged teal, gadwalls, shovelers, and ruddy ducks as well. These last three species traditionally have bred mainly west of the Mississippi, but are now becoming more common as breeders along the Atlantic coast.

Of all the ducks that nest in or visit the refuge, the little ruddy duck may be the most captivating. In spring, the male has a chestnut body, black crown, and white cheeks, and the colorful breeding attire also includes his bill, which is bright blue. Both the male and female ruddy have distinctive long, stiff tails which are often held straight up in the air. During his courtship display, the male raises and spreads his tail, and at the same time produces bubbles by expelling air trapped under his breast feathers. Although the ruddy duck is not a com-

Snow geese and "blue geese," Brigantine National Wildlife Refuge  *Courtesy Brigantine National Wildlife Refuge Staff*

mon breeder here, the pools along this section of the road are the best place to witness this strange display.

A little more than a mile beyond the observation tower, the road turns to follow the eastern edge of East Pool. Another ¾ mile and the road turns again, this time running parallel to Perch Cove to the right. Stretching out to the north and east are 16,000 acres of refuge salt marsh and bays which provide winter habitat for American brant, a small goose seldom found far from the ocean. Like the snow goose, it breeds on the Arctic tundra and winters on a small strip of the Atlantic coast from New Jersey to North Carolina.

Less than twenty years ago, the brant was faced with near extinction because of the almost complete destruction of its winter forage. The brant had traditionally fed almost exclusively on eelgrass, a ribbonlike marine plant, while in its winter quarters. Around 1930, a blight struck the eelgrass, and within a few years most of it had disappeared from the waters of the northeastern seaboard.

Food-habit studies of the brant after 1932 show that this adaptable goose made a tremendous dietary change in response to the decline of its preferred winter forage. Beginning at that time, a marine algae called sea lettuce made up about ¾ of the brant's diet, and now, while the eelgrass beds are still recovering, this plant continues to be an extremely important winter food for the brant.

The road passes the cross dike, then swings right before turning to follow the northern edge of the freshwater pool. Bits of cattail marsh flank the left side of the road here, and these harbor a variety of wildlife. Muskrat feed on the cattail rootstocks and tubers, while ducks, redwing blackbirds, and grackles nest among the tall, flexible leaves. Weasels prowl through them, hunting for meadow voles, and mink search the cattail hummocks for mice, frogs, and snakes.

On the other side of the road there is more salt marsh, broken by tidal creeks and mud flats. At low tide this is a good place to see fiddler crabs, which make their burrows in the banks of these tidal inlets. These crabs are hunted by glossy ibis, which can be seen here in large numbers in spring and summer, probing the mud with their long, downturned bill. The ibis is a strikingly colored bird, with rich chestnut plumage and iridescent green wings. Clapper rails, another wading bird that relishes fiddler crabs, nest along here, but these secretive birds are rarely seen.

Another ½ mile further, as the road nears the end of the pool, be on the lookout for peregrine falcons. Since 1976, Cornell University has released twenty young peregrines at Brigantine as part of its program to revive the population of this magnificent bird. The large raised platform that can be seen off to the left is one of the release sites, and it was here in the summer of 1980 that the first pair of captive bred peregrines successfully raised their own chick.

Just before the road swings to the left, there is a large excavation on the right; sand and gravel from this excavation were used to construct the dikes over which you have been walking. The trees on the bluff created by the removal of this material frequently serve as roosts for bald eagles. December is the most likely month to see bald eagles here, but they are occasionally seen during January and February.

The road is now firmly on dry land, but even here the water birds dot the landscape. The grassy fields to the left of the road are a favorite grazing area for Canada geese. Beyond these fields, the road leads into deciduous woods, and ½ mile further, reaches the parking area.

# Cape May

Red-tailed hawk, Cape May Point

# 24. Cape May City

Distance: 2½ miles (Easy)
Walking time: 3 hours
Directions: Take the Garden State Parkway south to the
end, then continue on Lafayette St. toward Cape May City.
Turn left on Schellinger St., then right onto Washington St.
Park at the Emlen Physick Estate (Cape May Museum),
1050 Washington St.

Considering the development of the New Jersey coast
from Asbury Park to Atlantic City, it is remarkable that the
historic seashore resort of Cape May survives. Though it
has changed a great deal in the past 100 years, Cape May
retains much of its nineteenth-century charm: its beautiful
Victorian buildings, many of which are still used for their
original purposes; its size, being still a walkable city; and
its slower, less commercial pace. A walking tour is the
most enjoyable way to see Cape May, and the one presented here is meant as a beginning for more extensive
rambles around this, the nation's oldest seashore resort.

The walk begins at the Emlen Physick house, which is
open to the public in the summer and on weekends in the
spring and fall. (The last two seasons are recommended
for this walk, since crowds of visitors are easily avoided.)
The peculiarities of the house's design—oversized dormers and chimneys that broaden as they extend above the
roof—are popularly attributed to the eccentricity of its
owner, Emlen Physick. However, these features were not
uncommon in nineteenth-century architecture. The architect, Frank Furness, built a number of houses of similar
design in Philadelphia at around the same time that he
designed the Physick house (1870).

From the Physick house, walk four blocks along Washington Street to Franklin Street and turn right. On the

168

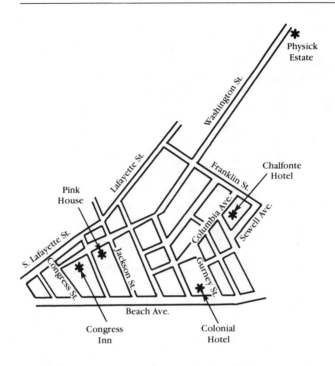

Physick
Estate

Washington St.

Franklin St.

Chalfonte
Hotel

Sewell Ave.

Lafayette St.

Columbia Ave.

Pink
House

S. Lafayette St.

Jackson St.

Gurney St.

Congress St.

Beach Ave.

Congress
Inn

Colonial
Hotel

left along the last block (720 Washington Street) is the
George Allen house, now called Victorian House. Built for
Allen, a Philadelphia merchant, in 1863–1864, the house
is one of the most elaborate that survives in Cape May.
Five-foot-high brackets support a gigantic roof, which in
turn supports a large, richly ornamented cupola. The opu-
lence outside is reflected within the house, where marble
fireplaces and foot-wide moldings delight the eye.

From Franklin Street, turn left onto Lafayette Street. The
bandstand on your left is not an authentic Victorian structure, but was built in 1974. Patterned after a bandstand in
Sefton Park in Liverpool, England, it was designed with
the structural elements of Victorian woodwork instead
of the cast-iron members that adorned the original. Almost directly across the street from the bandstand is the

*Cape May City* 169

Cape May Island Presbyterian Church, whose Georgian-vernacular facade contrasts with the unusual onion-domed, vaguely oriental cupola that towers above the building. Erected in 1853, the building served the congregation until 1898, when a new church was built; today, the Cape May Community Center is located here.

Just past the community center, turn left onto Jackson Street, and then almost immediately turn right onto Washington Street. Ahead lies the impressive Congress Hall and the row of lovely homes along Congress Place. Before you reach them, note the pink building on the left at the corner of Perry and Washington. This is the Eldridge Johnson house, now called the Pink House, which was built around 1880. The Pink House is probably the most elaborately decorated cottage in Cape May, its gingerbread woodwork looking like a huge veil draped in front of the building.

Crossing Perry Street, you reach Congress Place. On the left looms Congress Hall, a large L-shaped hotel facing the ocean. This building is actually the third on this site to have that name; the first, built around 1812, was one of the earliest hotels in Cape May. Rebuilt and modernized in the 1850s, Congress Hall was destroyed in the 1878 fire that burned thirty acres of the city, and then was rebuilt again in 1879.

Across the street are three homes built about the same time as the new Congress Hall—in fact, these homes are located on the site of the old hotel, which after the fire was relocated closer to the ocean. The middle building, the Joseph Evans house (identified by a black cast-iron widow's walk), was designed by Stephen Decatur Button, Cape May's most prolific and noted architect. Between 1863 and 1893, Button designed more than forty of the resort's buildings. His impact on the architecture of the town goes beyond the buildings he designed, however, since many of the local builders copied his work quite closely.

At the end of the block lies the E. C. Knight house, which may also have been designed by Button. Knight was one of the many influential Philadelphians who summered in Cape May—these merchants and bankers, lured by booming land values as much as by the sand and sea, directed much of the town's economic and physical growth. To a considerable extent this growth, like that in any resort town, has been dependent on the type of transportation available to potential visitors. Located at the confluence of the Atlantic Ocean and the Delaware River, Cape May was in the early 1800s only a river cruise from Philadelphia, and a relatively short distance (across Delaware Bay) from such urban centers as Washington, D.C. and Baltimore. In the middle of the 1800s steamboats and then trains kept Cape May within reach, although the railroad had reached Atlantic City before Cape May, and that resort's growth began to eclipse Cape May's around 1862.

As you turn right onto Congress Street, note the twin cottages straight ahead. Built around 1850 for two brothers, Joseph and John Steiner, these two buildings were among the first summer cottages built in Cape May. Up until 1850, tourists usually depended on hotels and rooming houses for their lodging, but the increase in personal wealth that began in the late 1800s led to a trend toward privately owned summer homes.

Turning left onto South Lafayette Street, you pass the Joseph Leedham house, located at the corner of South Lafayette and Congress streets. Round fish-scale-shingled towers, boldly projecting bays, and a complex asymmetry distinguish the house as being of the style known as Queen Anne. In many Cape May buildings of the 1870s and 1880s the Queen Anne influence appeared mainly in the form of towers added to conventional summer cottages, but the Leedham house, designed by Philadelphia architect Charles Collum in 1883, integrates many Queen Anne fashions into the overall building.

E. C. Knight house, Cape May City

Turn left onto Windsor Street and follow it out to
Beach Avenue. As you turn left onto Beach, you pass the
Windsor Hotel, which was built the same year as the new
Congress Hall. The L-shaped plan of both hotels gives the
maximum number of rooms an ocean view.

The construction of Beach Avenue and a boardwalk in
1869 were important developments in Cape May's history,
as they assured access to the ocean for the general public. Before the road and nearby buildings could be constructed, however, sand dunes had to be leveled and large
areas of wetland filled in. These dunes and marshes once
served as buffers against the fierce storms that ravaged
this area periodically, and with their destruction, the
waves whipped up by northeasters were free to batter the
growing resort town. Most recently, a storm in October

1980 caused hundreds of thousands of dollars worth of damage to property along the beachfront.

At the corner of Beach Avenue and Ocean Street, you pass the Colonial Hotel. Built in 1894, the Colonial was considered extremely modern in its time, featuring steam heat, gaslights, electric bells for room service, and the very first elevator in Cape May. Like the Windsor and the Congress Hall, it also advertised "superb ocean views from nearly every room."

Turn left onto Gurney Street; the houses along the left side of the street were designed by Button in 1871 and were collectively christened Stockton Place, in honor of the Stockton Hotel across the street. Although they are fairly typical Cape May cottages, some of the buildings are distinguished by their elaborate wood ornamentation. The Baldt house, located at 26 Gurney Street, retains all of its original woodwork, including the large wooden acroterion atop the roof peak. Others of the cottages have been modified a great deal: gingerbread has been removed, porches have been simplified, and shingles have been changed. The cottage next to the Baldt house has been almost totally rebuilt into a 1920s shingle-style house; its tall, narrow proportions and gable angles, however, identify it unmistakably as one of the original Stockton Place cottages.

At the end of Stockton Place is the fantastic John B. McCreary house (now The Abbey, a guest house). In 1869 McCreary, a wealthy coal baron and politician, commissioned Button to design a summer villa for him in Cape May. The result was a building so unusual that the *Cape May Ocean Wave* was prompted to comment on its style: "Elizabethan, Gothic, and Doric and a description of it so as to convey an idea of what it looks like would occupy more space than we have at our disposal this week." An imposing tower, stenciled and ruby glass windows, and the repetition of the Gothic arch in the doors, windows, and porch brackets are among the features that distinguish the McCreary house.

Turn right on Columbia Avenue, passing the Victorian mansion (now the Mainstay Inn) on the left. Originally known as Jackson's Clubhouse, the building is another Button design, built in 1872 for Col. Charles Jackson, a wealthy gambler from New York. Its stately porch, large veranda, and pilastered cupola distinguish it outside. Inside, the house is even more handsome, graced by fourteen-foot ceilings, ornate plaster moldings, and elaborate chandeliers. Many of the original furnishings remain in the house, and these can be seen on the guided tours which are offered from May through November.

Turn left at Jackson's Clubhouse and then right on Hughes Street, passing a number of houses built between 1868 and 1872. The first, the Joseph Hall house (645 Hughes), has distinctive vinelike woodwork on the main dormer, but is otherwise somewhat plain. The J. Stratton Ware house (653 Hughes) is much more elaborate, with ornate barge boards, incised carvings, and acroteria crowning the dormers.

To return to the Physick house and your car, turn left on Franklin Street, then right onto Washington Street.

# 25. Cape May Point State Park

Distance: 2 miles (Easy)
Walking time: 1 hour
Directions: Take the Garden State Parkway south to the ·
end, then continue on Lafayette St. to Cape May City. Turn
right on Perry, which then becomes West Sunset Blvd.,
and go 2 miles to Lighthouse Ave. The park entrance is ¾
mile down on the left.

For many people, Cape May is synonymous with birds.
Since records were first maintained, over 360 species of
birds have been recorded at Cape May, making it one of
the most famous places to observe birds in all of North
America. Particularly spectacular at Cape May is the autumn hawk migration: from early September to late
November, hundreds of hawks can be seen each day, and
on good days, hawks number in the thousands. In 1977, a
total of 81,597 hawks were seen from the observation
area at Cape May Point State Park, a national record for
the most hawks recorded from a single point during an
autumn migration.

Cape May is a long, narrow extension of the Outer
Coastal Plain, and is bordered by Delaware Bay on the
west and the Atlantic Ocean on the east. Because many
birds are hesitant to cross large stretches of open water,
Cape May's geography makes it a natural funnel, catching
southbound landbirds and channeling them to its termi-
nus at Cape May Point. A walk through Cape May Point
State Park then, no matter what the season, is highlighted
by the abundant and varied birdlife, but you need not be
a birdwatcher to enjoy this unique area.

From the parking lot, walk to the trail entrance, which
is marked by a sign. The trail is flanked by phragmites,
groundsel-tree, elderberry, wax myrtle, and bayberry.

175

These last two shrubs are closely related and are similar
in appearance: both have egg-shaped, slightly toothed
leaves that have minute resin dots on the surface. These
resin dots account for the strong scent of the leaves when
they are crushed. Wax myrtle's leathery leaves stay on the
plant all year long, while the bayberry is deciduous; it is
also distinguished by being less shrubby in its growth
habit.

The most conspicuous similarity in the two plants is
their small, wax-covered nutlets, or berries, which hug
the twigs. These berries were commonly harvested during
colonial days to make scented candles, as some enterpris-
ing people still do today. (A pound of nutlets immersed in
hot water yields four ounces of wax.) Today, most of the
harvesting is done by myrtle warblers (now officially
known as yellow-rumped warblers) who during their fall
migration light by the thousands to feed on the bayber-
ries. The myrtle warbler can be seen here through Janu-

ary and February, as it is the only warbler that regularly spends the winter this far north.

The principal tree in the open sections of the park is the eastern red cedar, which is recognized by its dry, papery bark that shreds to reveal the reddish heartwood below. Its dark green needles are of two different kinds: some are sharply pointed, while others, particularly on older trees, are flattened and overlapping. The fruit is a hard, bluish berry that is covered with a whitish bloom. The red cedar is the most widely distributed conifer of tree size in the eastern United States, growing under a wide variety of soil and climatic conditions. The tenacity that makes it such an aggressive colonizer of abandoned fields further north serves it as well on the dry, wind-swept coastal sands here.

The trail, marked by red and blue blazes, passes a persimmon tree that is laden with fruit in the fall, and then forks. Bear left here into the red-blazed trail, which leads to a boardwalk. The boardwalk comes upon a pond that has filled in with vegetation to become an open meadow ringed by tall phragmites. This is a good spot to glance up, as sharp-shinned and marsh hawks stream by overhead. The number of hawks depends to a large degree on the weather conditions. Generally, good hawk flights follow the passage of a cold front, when a low-pressure system moves off the New England coast, while a high-pressure system moves out of Canada. Such a weather system produces northwest winds, which blow inland migrants toward the coast, concentrating them in the numbers that make hawk watching at Cape May so spectacular.

Along the following section of boardwalk there is a small detour to the left which leads to a platform overlooking a freshwater pond. Painted turtles sun themselves here while mallards and black ducks float lazily along the surface. If you look very carefully you may see a least bittern as it skulks through the cattails and reed grass that ring the outer edge of the pond. This small, extremely secretive heron has a blackish back and conspicuous buff wing patches and underparts.

The trail passes into a wooded area, where it joins the blue trail; turn left here. After passing back into the open, the trail enters a wooded section again, where sweet gum and sassafras are the principal trees. Sassafras is easily identified by its sweet-smelling leaves, which occur in three different shapes. Most commonly the leaves are oval, but they are less commonly divided into three lobes; occasionally they are two lobed or mitten shaped. On older trees the bark is a deeply furrowed orange brown, and the new shoots are bright yellowish green. In fall, the leaves of the sassafras turn brilliant colors, ranging from yellow through orange and even pink.

After about ¼ mile the trail emerges into an open field. In the fall, the Cape May Bird Observatory, the research arm of the New Jersey Audubon Society, uses this field as part of its banding operation. If you remain hidden along the edge of the woods, you'll see what appears to be an injured pigeon flapping about on the ground. The pigeon is actually tethered to serve as a lure for hawks flying overhead, who swoop down to capture the "injured" bird, only to be caught in the observatory's nets. These hawks are then marked with a small aluminum leg band, which will serve to provide information for bird migration and population studies should the hawk be recaptured at a future date.

The trail passes back into the woods, which on days with very strong northwest winds, may be filled with half a dozen hawks perched quietly in the black cherry trees. On such extremely windy days, many hawks are reluctant to fly, and take cover in wooded sections like this one. The trail shortly leaves the woods and crosses a marshy area covered by phragmites before returning through a wooded section.

178  *Cape May Point State Park*

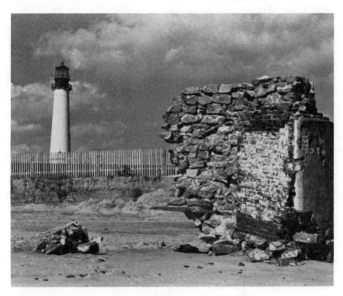

Cape May lighthouse with ruins of old lighthouse in foreground, Cape May State Park

About ⅛ mile into the woods, there is a short detour to
the left to an observation platform overlooking a small
pond. The pond is again ringed by phragmites, but just
beyond is a small cattail marsh. In spring, this marsh is
alive with the sights and sounds of redwing blackbirds,
who build their cup-shaped nests amid the tall cattail
leaves. The territorial males can be seen flying above the
marsh calling loudly while displaying their brilliant red
shoulder patches or epaulets. These red epaulets contrast
sharply with the all-black plumage of the rest of the redwing's body, and like many such color patches, they serve
as a means of communication. When the male redwing
flashes his brightly colored epaulets, they are as effective
as his throaty call in advertising his presence to compet-
ing males.

Directly in front of the platform can be seen the cone-shaped house of a muskrat. The muskrat house is built of piled-up cattail stalks, roots, plant remains, and mud which is dug from the area around the house foundation. The mainly nocturnal muskrat is active throughout the year and is sometimes seen during the daytime building houses, swimming, or sunning itself. The stems, leaves, and roots of many marsh plants, particularly cattail, form the bulk of the muskrat's diet.

Just after the trail leaves the woods, it reaches an intersection with a yellow-blazed trail; turn right here. The trail follows through more phragmites before reaching a brackish pond. Here salt water has invaded, and instead of being surrounded by cattail and reed grass, the marshy area around the pond consists of spike grass and salt-meadow grass.

When you reach the dune, turn right and follow the beach. This is a good area to look for Cape May diamonds, actually quartz pebbles that have been polished smooth by thousands of years of weathering and abrasion. The "diamonds" vary from the size of tiny peas to, quite rarely, the size of a chicken's egg, and are usually colorless, though some are tinted yellow or amber. Cape May diamonds are thought to be derived from the sands and gravels deposited throughout southern New Jersey during the Pleistocene. These sands and gravels are largely stained yellow from limonite, but some of the pebbles from deposits that have been washed into the sea have had this limonite coating removed by natural abrasion. (Limonite-stained sands can be seen along exposed sections of this beach.)

As you walk along the dunes, keep an eye out for migrating falcons: kestrels, merlins, and peregrines. Unlike the buteos and accipiter hawks, these strong fliers with scimitar-shaped wings prefer to migrate along the coast. The sight of a feisty merlin or peregrine winging low over the dunes in pursuit of a migrating shorebird is a sight not soon forgotten.

The large concrete structure being undermined by the sea is the remains of a United States army artillery unit built during World War II. The ocean has had severe effects on the dunes near here as well. Just beyond the bunker lies an area of sand dune which was blown out during a northeast storm in the fall of 1980. The fresh-water pond formerly protected from the sea was invaded by salt water, making the pond brackish in some sections.

Continue down the beach until you reach the ruins of an old lighthouse foundation. The history of lighthouses at Cape May Point tells much about the continued encroachment of the sea. The first lighthouse was built in 1823 and was located about ⅓ of a mile south of the present lighthouse. This was removed in 1847 to this site, but in 1859 the sea had again encroached, and the lighthouse was moved to its present location near the entrance to the park.

From here, walk back along the beach a few hundred yards to the trail that returns to the parking lot. If it's a good day, you might like to stop at the observation platform located near the parking area. From the first of September through the last of November, observers from the Cape May Bird Observatory are here counting hawks, and an hour or so spent with them can be an excellent introduction to hawk identification.

**Geologic Timetable**

**Glossary**

**Identification Index**

# Geologic Timetable

| Era | Period | Epoch | *Millions of years ago* |
|-----|--------|-------|------------------------|
| Cenozoic | Quaternary | Recent | |
| | | Pleistocene (The Great Ice Age) | 2.5 |
| | Tertiary | Pliocene | 7 |
| | | Miocene | 26 |
| | | Oligocene | 38 |
| | | Eocene | 54 |
| | | Paleocene | 65 |
| Mesozoic | Cretaceous | | |
| | | | 136 |
| | Jurassic | | |
| | | | 190 |
| | Triassic | | |
| | | | 225 |
| Paleozoic | Permian | | 280 |
| | Pennsylvanian | | 320 |
| | Mississippian | | 345 |
| | Devonian | | 395 |
| | Silurian | | |

| Global geological/biological events | New Jersey rocks |
|---|---|
| Many large Ice Age mammals become extinct. | Present-day stream deposits, beaches. |
| Continental glaciation; origin of human beings. | Glacial deposits in north; yellow gravels in central and south. |
| Mammals at height. Rocky Mts. born (75 million years ago). | Unconsolidated sediments of the N.J. coastal plain. |
| Extinction of dinosaurs; origin of birds and mammals. | Unconsolidated sediments of northwestern part of the N.J. coastal plain. |
| Breakup of Pangaea; N.A., Africa, and Eurasia drift apart. | Palisades disturbance. |
| Rise of dinosaurs. | Red shales, sandstones, argillites, basalt extrusives, and diabase intrusives of the Newark basin. |
| Origin of reptiles. | Not present in N.J. |
| Great fern forests; coal deposits of Pennsylvania. | Not present in N.J. |
| | Not present in N.J. |
| Origin of amphibians; age of fishes. | Upper Delaware limestone, Bearfort Mt. conglomerate. |
| First land plants. | High Falls sandstone in northwest N.J., conglomerate in Green Pond Valley (Morris and Passaic counties). |

| Era | Period | Epoch | Millions of years ago |
|-----|--------|-------|----------------------|
| | Ordovician | | 500 |
| | Cambrian | | 570 |
| Precambrian | | | |

| Global geological/biological events | New Jersey rocks |
|---|---|
| Extensive warm, shallow seas; trilobites. | Shales and limestones of Kittatinny Ridge. Limestone and sandstone in Sussex and Warren counties. |
| Oldest fossils (3 billion years old). Oldest rocks (3.7 billion years old). | Gneiss and other metamorphic rocks, Franklin marble in N.J. Highlands. |

# Glossary

*accipiter*: any of a group of hawks characterized by long tails, short, rounded wings, and low darting flight

*alluvial*: soil deposited by running water

*alternate* (leaves, buds): not opposite, but arranged singly at intervals along twigs

*argillite*: a compact, clay-containing rock having no slaty cleavage

*barrier beach*: a low island of sand built by waves, parallel to the shore, and separated from it by a lagoon or shallow bay

*basalt*: a dark gray to black fine-grained igneous rock

*bedrock*: the solid rock underlying unconsolidated surface materials (i.e. soil)

*bog*: a poorly drained, acidic wetland, rich in organic remains (plant residues)

*boreal*: northern

*bottomland*: low-lying, moist area along streams and rivers

*bract*: a modified leaf that encloses another structure, usually a flower

*buteo*: any of a group of hawks characterized by broad wings and tail, and soaring flight

*canopy*: the uppermost layer of foliage in a forest

*carapace*: the horny or bony protective covering over the back of an animal (e.g. a turtle's shell)

*catkin*: cluster of tiny flowers or fruits, usually fuzzy and caterpillar shaped (such as those of willows)

*climax*: the final stage in the succession of plants in a particular setting of soil and climate

*compound* (leaf): one composed of separate leaflets, each of which usually looks like a single leaf (ash, hickory)

*conglomerate*: a sedimentary rock composed of rounded fragments varying from small pebbles to large boulders within a matrix of sandstone

*conifer*: a member of an order (Coniferales) of trees and shrubs having evergreen foliage and bearing seeds in a cone (pine, cedar, etc.)

188

*deciduous*: a tree that is not an evergreen, but loses its leaves seasonally, usually in autumn

*diabase*: a finely crystalline igneous rock

*dominant*: any plant that predominates in a community by height, size, and number

*dorsal*: related to the back of an animal

*drift*: unsorted rock debris deposited by a glacier

*endemic*: limited in distribution to a particular region or habitat

*epoch*: a division of geologic time less than a period

*estuary*: the lower end of a river that meets the sea

*extrusive*: formed by crystallization of lava poured out at the earth's surface

*fault*: a fracture in the earth's crust accompanied by lateral displacements of the opposing sides of the fracture

*floodplain*: level land that is seasonally inundated by floodwaters

*floret*: a single small flower within a group of similar small flowers

*flyway*: an established air route of migratory birds

*fold*: a bend produced in rock by geologic forces

*formation*: any consecutive series of rock layers homogeneous enough to be a unit

*fungus*: any of a large group of plants, including mushrooms, molds, and the like, that lack chlorophyll and reproduce by means of spores

*genus*: a group of species sufficiently closely related to be given the same (Latin) generic name

*glacier*: a large body of ice spreading outward on a land surface

*gneiss*: a coarse-grained metamorphic rock with a banded appearance

*granite*: a very hard igneous rock consisting mainly of quartz

*habitat*: the place in which a plant or animal naturally lives and grows

*heath*: any of a family of plants that thrive on open, barren, often acidic soil

*herbaceous*: plants having little or no woody tissue and persisting usually for a single growing season

*hyphae*: the individual tubelike threads of a fungus

*igneous*: pertaining to rock formed by the process of hot magma cooling above or below the earth's surface *insectivorous*: depending on insects for food

*intermittent stream*: one that dries up seasonally

*lenticel*: a circular or stripelike corky spot on the bark originating as a breathing pore

*lichen*: a plant made up of an alga and fungus growing in symbiotic association

*limestone*: rock formed chiefly by accumulation of organic remains (e.g. shells, coral)

*limonite*: a compound of iron oxide and water

*lithify*: to become rock

*lobed* (leaf): divided into rounded, incompletely separated sections

*magma*: molten rock material within the earth

*magnetite*: a black iron oxide mineral

*mantle*: unconsolidated material overlying bedrock

*metamorphic*: rock that has been deformed by intense heat and pressure within the earth's crust

*microclimate*: the uniform local climate of a small site or habitat

*midden*: a refuse heap

*moraine*: an accumulation of earth and stones carried and finally deposited by a glacier

*nymph*: a larva of an insect

*opposite* (leaves, buds): in opposing pairs

*outcrop*: an exposure of bare rock; a place where underlying rock protrudes from the soil

*peat*: an accumulation of partially decomposed organic material

*peneplain*: a large expanse of gently rolling land

*period*: a division of geologic time longer than an epoch and included in an era

*pH*: the measure of acidity or alkalinity

*pinnae*: leaflets of a pinnate leaf or frond

*pinnate*: having the leaflets placed at opposite points on the stem

*primaries*: the principal flight feathers of a bird's wing

*quartz*: a transparent or colored mineral ($SiO_2$) occurring in hexagonal crystals or crystalline masses

*quartzite*: a compact granular rock composed of quartz and derived from sandstone by metamorphism

*raptor*: a bird of prey

*relict*: a persistent remnant of an otherwise extinct flora or fauna

*riparian*: of or relating to or living on the bank of a river

*rosette*: a cluster of leaves in crowded circles or spirals

*samara*: a dry, usually one-seeded winged fruit (e.g. those of ash or maple)

*sandstone*: a sedimentary rock usually made up of quartz sand

*scree*: rock fragments at the base of a cliff

*scute*: a small horny or bony plate

*sedimentary rock*: rock formed of mechanical, chemical, or organic sediment

*shale*: an easily fragmented rock formed by the consolidation of clay, mud, or silt

*sill*: a body of igneous rock injected while molten into some other type of rock

*sinus*: a deep indentation in the margin of a leaf

*slate*: a dense, fine-grained metamorphic rock usually produced by compression of shale

*snag*: the standing remains of a dead or dying tree

*spadix*: a fleshy spike in which florets are embedded

*spathe*: a large bract around a flower

*spore*: the reproductive body (asexual) of a primitive plant or fungus

*stamen*: the male or pollen-bearing part of a flower

*striation*: scratch made in rock by glacial movement of rock material

*succession*: the natural process by which plant communities replace one another

*talons*: claws

*talus*: rock fragments at the base of a cliff

*taproot*: a primary root that grows straight down

*tendril*: a clasping, twining, slender outgrowth of the stem

*till*: unstratified, unsorted rocks, gravel, and debris deposited by a glacier

*traprock*: various dark-colored, fine-grained igneous rocks (such as basalt or diabase)

*understory*: the layer of forest growth below the canopy

# Identification Index

| | |
|---|---|
| Locust, black | Palisades Interstate Park |
| Maple: | |
| red | Cheesequake State Park |
| silver | Delaware and Raritan Canal State Park |
| striped | High Point State Park |
| sugar | Skylands Botanical Gardens |
| Oak: | |
| black | Herrontown Woods |
| chestnut | Ramapo Mountain State Forest |
| red | Herrontown Woods |
| scrub | Lebanon State Forest |
| Persimmon | Rancocas State Park |
| Pine: | |
| pitch | Lebanon State Forest |
| red | Skylands Botanical Gardens |
| Virginia | Rancocas State Park |
| white | Skylands Botanical Gardens |
| Prickly pear | Gateway National Recreation Area |
| Red cedar | Cape May Point State Park |
| Sassafras | Cape May Point State Park |
| Sheep laurel | Lebanon State Forest |
| Sumac: | |
| staghorn | Palisades Interstate Park |
| winged | Island Beach State Park |
| Sweet bay | Wharton State Forest |
| Sweet gum | Skylands Botanical Gardens |
| Sweet pepperbush | Wharton State Forest |
| Sycamore | Delaware and Raritan Canal State Park |
| Tulip tree | Skylands Botanical Gardens |
| Umbrella magnolia | Rancocas State Park |
| Virginia creeper | Island Beach State Park |
| Witch hazel | Stokes State Forest |